NO ONE KNEW

My Emotional Journey of Being Married to a Sociopath & How I Learned to Heal

RENEE OLIVIER

No One Knew

Library of Congress Control Number 2020909528

Cover Design by Goodlife Guide

ISBN 978-0-578-68852-7 (pbk.)
ISBN 978-0-578-68856-5 (ebook)

Printed in the United States of America

ACKNOWLEDGMENTS

This book is dedicated to my children, who took much of this journey with me. Their strength and love have lifted me out of the many fears I faced while weathering a dark storm at such a difficult time in our lives. I love you both more than you will ever know.

To my husband, I am so thankful that I have you in my corner pushing me when I am ready to give up. All the good that comes from this book, I look forward to sharing with you. You are my hero. Thanks for not just believing in me but for your enduring love and knowing that I could do this. I love you more!

Lastly, thank you to everyone who helped me be a voice for others by writing this book, my family and friends who shared their thoughts of encouragement, and to the online writing communities who offered their support and guidance.

Contents

Introduction

Many people are unaware of what a sociopath is and what they are capable of. Some may feel that something is off about their partner but don't even realize that they are in a relationship with a very dangerous and inherently evil person. How do I know? Because that was me. I had no idea what traits and characteristics defined a sociopath. I always thought they were the serial killer types you see on television. That is far from the truth. The ultimate goal of writing this book is to hopefully help someone else who may be in a relationship with a sociopath. It delves into my personal story that "NO ONE KNEW" and how I learned to heal and love myself again.

SOCIOPATH—THE MAN BEHIND THE MASK

I am using the word "*Man*" because I am referring to my ex-husband, however, sociopaths can also be women as well. I am not a doctor or psychologist; therefore, I am not giving medical advice or psychotherapy of any kind. This book is strictly my story on what happened to me. I know what it feels like to be the victim of a sociopath. Wanting so badly to speak to someone else but scared that no one would believe my account of things that happened because my story was so bizarre with what my ex-husband did to keep his power and control over me.

I suffered years of verbal abuse, which left me emotionally and physically scarred. No one knew what I went through, except my children who endured a great deal listening to his wild outbursts and being a witness to his irresponsible behavior. This book is important for me to put out in the world, and I can only hope that it makes a difference to someone out there that feels alone because no one can truly understand what someone is going through that's experiencing a sociopath's wrath. I do.

DEFINING A SOCIOPATH—WHO THEY ARE

A sociopath is a term used to describe someone with antisocial personality disorder (ASPD). They lack empathy, particularly an inability to feel remorse for their actions. They pour on the charm and then can turn at the drop of a hat and be deceitful, aggressive, and violent with their words in a threatening way. They are hostile, irresponsible, impulsive, and get involved in risky behavior. They need instant gratification and have little concern for the safety of others or themselves. This all stems from a lack of self-worth within themselves. They think they're above everyone else to the outside world, and they tend to blame other people for their circumstances.

SOME SYMPTOMS OF ASPD CAN INCLUDE

1. Being "cold" by not showing emotions or investment in the lives of others

2. Using humor, intelligence, or charisma to manipulate others

3. Not learning from mistakes

4. Having a sense of superiority and strong, unwavering opinions

5. Attempting to control others by intimidating or threatening them

6. Threatening suicide without ever acting on these threats

7. Not being able to keep positive friendships or relationships

8. Lying, cheating or deceiving others

9. Breaking rules without regard for the consequences

10. Destroying things that belong to themselves or others

Being with a sociopath is like being with a person behind the mask. I have learned a great deal about sociopathic behavior, but mostly, I have learned a great deal about myself. My ex-husband was well aware of the pain he inflicted on me; he liked hurting me to the point he felt powerful. I was a nurturing mother, loyal in my relationship with him, compassionate and empathetic. I learned that sociopaths target these qualities in someone. They can mask their persona as your soulmate, they suck you into their world, and then once they have you where they want you, they attack.

Even though there are other stories from experts and therapists on sociopath's traits and characteristics, I truly believe it takes someone that has lived it every day, sometimes for years, to know what they are capable of and the trauma it can cause on your self-worth. I think there has been so little research done and that most people can't identify a sociopath and are unsure of what is happening to them at times.

It's often our own emotions that first tell us to beware, but your brain wants to believe everything they tell you. Many people marry sociopaths even though they saw some warning signs and deep down they knew something wasn't right. I did exactly that. I married my ex-husband, Joe, after five years of living together, even though I knew how volatile he could be. I was emotionally paralyzed by him.

He had me right where he wanted me—under his control as his victim. In my story, I use the term "gaslighting" which is a form of psychological manipulation that my ex-husband used on me. The word gaslighting gets its name from the 1944 movie called *Gaslight*, in which a man manipulates his wife to the point where she thinks she is losing her mind.

Gaslighting is planting seeds of doubt in a targeted individual, making them question their own memory, perception, or sanity. It is a form of emotional abuse. It can happen very gradually in a relationship. Over time, these abusive patterns continue and a victim can become confused, anxious, isolated, and depressed, and they can lose all sense of what is actually happening. Then they start relying on the abusive partner more and more to define their reality, which creates a very difficult situation to leave the relationship.

Gaslighting gives the abusive partner a lot of power, and with my ex-husband, he was all about power and control. He broke my ability to trust my own perception, which is why I stayed in the relationship for eight years. Gaslighting is very common in sociopaths and narcissists. They want to win and remain in control and they will succeed at all costs. Joe charmed me, manipulated me, isolated me, verbally abused me, and blamed me for every situation that didn't go his way.

If you are uncomfortable and believe someone may be gaslighting you, trust your intuitive feelings—that "gut feeling" that tells you not to ignore the red flags that are waving wildly right in front of you. A red flag is merely your intuition piecing things together, picking up on bad vibes, abnormal behavior, and things that don't add up right. I now look at red flags as a guide and no longer ignore them as I use to do so often.

Knowing what to look for and the warning signs of someone that is exhibiting sociopathic behavior may help you decide to walk away. According to Harvard psychologist, Martha Stout, author of "The Sociopath Next

Door[1]," *one in every twenty-five people is a sociopath.* They walk among us, like a wolf in sheep's clothing.

The sociopath carefully crafts his relationships so that he can get his partner to do his bidding, whatever that is. He will start off having you believe you're his soulmate and treat you like a queen, only so he can get away with sneakily treating you like a pawn. Once he identifies your weak spots, he will use them to manipulate you.

For eight years, I was lied to, emotionally abused, threatened, and intimated by a man who all the while professed his undying love for me. This book is a memoir. I wrote it because I felt I had to share my story and be a voice for others that may be too scared to speak up for themselves, as I was once that person. I've been faithful to my memory, but my subjects may remember things differently as I intend no harm to anyone. For privacy concerns, I have modified names and specific places of reference but not the narrative.

I recently moved to the Midwest and have found great joy in the majestic lifestyle that country living offers. The change has done my heart good. It was here where I finally felt at peace and I was able to embrace my fear while finding my sense of courage to write this book. I have also found love again and happily married to my best friend, who is loving, kind, and brings so much joy to my life. The hardest thing for me once I left Joe was to trust another person. I took time to heal and found myself again along the way. What I recognized through this whole experience is that I had to learn to trust myself and that the secret of true happiness came from within me.

The one person you need to love every day is "You." I realized that my ex-husband taught me the most important lesson of my life—to trust myself. I moved on from the gaslighting and the abuse, followed my heart, and focused on things I loved. Ending a relationship with a sociopath is only part of the journey. The next step of healing is loving yourself. Starting over and finding you again. To learn to trust yourself.

My sincere hope is that my story can help someone else involved with a sociopath to understand that they are not alone and how they can protect themselves and find courage, strength, and love after leaving the relationship. Months after my divorce was final, I was asked by a friend if I had met someone else. I remember smiling and saying, "Yes— I met me.

Chapter One

The Soulmate Sociopath

When I was a little girl, I dreamed of marrying my prince charming. I even dreamt of his undying love for me. The kind of love that would fight evil villains and slay fire breathing dragons. We would go on to live happily ever after. I believed in the pureness of love then and still do to this day. I wanted my happy ending. I never could have imagined what was to come.

My first husband, Samuel, and I were married for twelve years, and we had two wonderful children. I was twenty-three, and my biological clock was ticking then. However, being young and still growing ourselves, we both grew apart, mainly from long work hours and being parents. We never really just spent quality time together, and unfortunately, our marriage suffered from it. We decided to separate amicably.

It was the first time in my life that I felt alone, and it felt strange, although my children lived with me most of the time. My son, Ryan, now ten years old, was a very spiritual child. He could shock you at times with the things he would say. We didn't attend church very often, but out of the blue, he would say a prayer around the dinner table that would make you tear up with his choice of words. I like to believe that the Lord was speaking through him. It made my heart soar.

My daughter, Emma, was always a happy child with a smile on her face. She could make other people smile with her genuine sweetness. She was three and a half years younger than Ryan and she looked up to him. He was always looking out for her. Growing up, my brother and I fought all the time like cats and dogs, so it was refreshing to see my children interact in a loving way towards one another.

Once we filed for divorce, I started selling homes in a new home community in Phoenix, Arizona, and then decided to move to the area from Prescott. I threw myself into my work, as I enjoyed assisting new home buyers with the purchase of their first home. Many times, I worked weekends and Ryan and Emma would spend the days with their father, who at the time was still commuting from Prescott. I was either at work or at home, and I eventually got to the point where I wanted to get out there and start dating again. It had been over thirteen years since I was single, and I wasn't sure what to expect, venturing out to the unknown and into the world of dating.

It terrified me to go to clubs or bars, as that really wasn't my scene, but then a friend told me I should sign up on a dating website. At least there, I could control who I spoke to and didn't have to be subjected to the pressure of getting to know someone in ten minutes, sitting face to face, only to realize there was no connection between us. Online dating sites were now the norm. Being on the single scene and putting my photo and profile information out there for all to see felt very awkward.

What I didn't realize is how time-consuming the dating site became. I went out on a few dates here and there, but I wasn't feeling a connection with anyone, that is until I met Joe. We chatted online for some time and found we had a great deal in common. He only lived a few streets away from me. I couldn't help but wonder if it was a sign and thought, *"I think I'm supposed to meet this man. What can it hurt?"*

I sensed it would be comfortable meeting him as I felt like I already knew him from our online chats. So, we decided to meet at a local restaurant a few days later. I remember feeling excited but very nervous. Was I ready for this? I really wasn't expecting much but I knew I enjoyed our conversations. I entered the restaurant and didn't see him at first. As I sat down in the lounge with my back facing the entrance, I heard a voice from behind that said, "Hello, beautiful."

My heart felt as if it was beating out of my chest as I turned around in anticipation. My first thought was, *"Wow, he's better looking in person than in his online profile photos."* Joe had a vibe about him that was charismatic and charming, a vibe that said, *"I can take on the world."* The way he made me laugh and his flirtatious nature made me feel alive. I felt myself slowly falling for him.

We talked for hours and stayed until the restaurant closed for the evening. I couldn't believe how fast time had gone by just enjoying each other's company. I was enamored by him. He played on my emotions and my heart and he was out to win. I was surprised to learn how much we had in common, or so I thought. We both had been through a divorce, and he had a daughter who was only two years younger than Emma. Her name was Hannah. He played on my sympathy about his short marriage to his ex-wife, Christy. He went on to explain that they had been dating three years prior, and she helped him through a difficult time from a past relationship.

He wanted to have children and knew he wasn't in love with Christy but only continued to date her because of her loyalty to him. Christy soon became pregnant and he knew he wanted to do the right thing for his unborn child, so he asked her to marry him soon after. He just wanted to make things right. He reasoned that he didn't want to bring a child into the world knowing that he didn't marry her mother. At the time, I thought this was noble of him but also a bit odd as I grew up believing you marry someone for love. Where was he expecting this marriage to go if he wasn't in love with Christy?

Two years later, the marriage ended in divorce after he said that he found medical bills of hers adding up to thousands of dollars. She had been hiding them from him, and for him, that was the last straw. I asked if she was sick or thought maybe she was just scared to tell him that something was wrong with her. He calmly told me that she had *Munchausen Syndrome*, which is a mental disorder in which she was faking an illness to gain attention and sympathy from him.

Joe told me then that he couldn't trust her and wasn't sure what she would do next, so he decided to end the marriage. His exact words to me were, "I didn't love her anyway." That would be the first of many red flags that I ignored. I felt sorry for him as he told me his story. He couldn't live with someone that lied to him and ultimately left him with thousands of dollars in medical bills. He made no attempt to mend their relationship from there. He was devastated when he was served divorce papers to find out that Christy was trying to take him to court to get as much money as she could from him.

Joe had his own business and she knew he did well for himself, so she went after him for half of his business, and that escalated into many arguments and threats over that time. He wanted to move on, which is what he was trying to do. Of course, my relationship with my children's father was amicable. We were supportive of one another in raising our children, and I felt grateful, especially after hearing Joe's story.

I was empathetic sitting there listening to Joe, which is why I believe I became his next target. He was reeling me in, and he was good at it. By the time we went on an official first date, he had me believing that we were soulmates. He enjoyed telling me that we were two pieces of a puzzle that fit together. He had found his missing piece and meeting me was the best thing that had ever happened to him. I believed him.

He seemed shaken as he told me about Christy and what she had done to him, and he was genuinely concerned for his daughter and what Christy might do to keep her away from him. She wanted full custody of Hannah, and he was going to fight to get joint custody. It wasn't fair to him or to Hannah. She needed him just as much as he needed her. How could he have been so mistreated by Christy? Why would she do that to him? The compassionate part of myself wanted to help. I warmed to Joe.

We connected and had so much in common. My heart went out to him, as he had lost his mother at a young age and I hadn't seen my own father throughout my childhood, so there was just an understanding we had for one another, or so I thought. Unbeknownst to me, I was already on his radar. I was empathetic, kind, and trusting, and I was paving the way to become his next victim.

Chapter Two

You Did What?

Looking back, I believe there were many factors that drew me to Joe. It wasn't just his heroic charm but his ability to be a leader. He was bold and exciting, he was always the life of the party, and he had his way in the bedroom. The sexual tension between us was undeniable, thrilling, and left me wanting more, at least back then. I loved being with him, and after I was introduced to his daughter, Hannah, I felt a natural motherly instinct to protect her as she ended up coming over to my house on many occasions since Joe had to work late on certain days. She and my daughter became fast friends. One evening Joe asked me to meet him for dinner at a local restaurant down the street.

He had a serious look on his face when I walked in and asked me to sit in the bar with him. Something told me that I was going to get a shock of some sort, but I sat down and waited for the bizarre story that was about to follow. He found it difficult to make eye contact as he took my hand

and turned to face me. "I don't know how to tell you this." I started feeling a bit like I could faint with the words of dread that I felt would be coursing through my body at any moment.

I was unprepared for the words that followed. "I have another child. She will soon be born, and the mother lives in San Antonio, Texas, and was someone I had a fling with after my divorce. She wouldn't consider an abortion, so I had a paternity test done just to see if the baby is mine and it is. I intend to try and get custody once the baby's a little older as the mother is a drug addict and her parents will have temporary custody of her. I understand if you want to walk away from all of this. I didn't tell you before because I was hoping you would understand and didn't want to lose you."

I felt as if someone had just hit me over the head, trying to comprehend the seriousness of his words as they washed over me. He stared straight at me until I managed to ask, "You did what? It was a lot to absorb. Here I was thinking he was going to call things off because he might have met someone else, but I didn't expect him to say that he had another child. What did this mean? Should I walk away? Should I be supportive that he cares enough about that baby to get custody of her?

Many men would probably just walk away from that situation, however, what really bothered me was the timeline. I met Joe in February of 2009 and in November of 2008, he had gone to Texas on business and met up with his good friend who introduced Joe to his new baby mama, Desiree, who apparently liked to party and experiment with drugs.

They were inseparable for the few weeks he was in San Antonio, and two months later, he received news from her that she was pregnant. That means, he knew that she was pregnant before meeting me in February. I felt this was unfair now after we started seriously dating. I had already invested myself and my children into his life. Then I thought about that unborn baby. If he didn't fight for custody, what would happen to her? Would she end up doing drugs or live a life on the streets?

Desiree had recently gone to jail for a drug charge, and what kind of life would that little girl have? On the other hand, if he got custody, she wouldn't have any kind of mother figure around. I felt for her, and she wasn't even born yet. The baby was due in August and every ounce of me fought to get up and walk away. To tell Joe to take a hike. I didn't want any drama or more added to my plate, but I didn't do any of that. Looking at him, he looked like a scared little boy trying to do the right thing.

I gathered my courage to speak without sounding condescending and said, "If the mother is addicted to drugs, you should fight to get custody of her. It's the right thing to do." He smiled, almost as if he knew that's what I was going to say. As time went by, things were good for a while, and then I lost my job in sales due to the turn of the housing market. People were panicked, and many backed out of their home purchases. I became scared. Where did I go from here? Unemployment wouldn't cover my rent and utilities. I started job hunting, and once I told Joe it was difficult finding another job, he suggested I move in with him.

He had a four-bedroom house with enough room for everyone, and he had hinted about me moving in with him on a few occasions. Just the week before, we were lying in his bed, and he had said he loved me for the first time. I was a bit startled by it, but it felt good to hear. It was so soon after getting a divorce but being the romantic I am, I believed him. Love knows no bounds or timing. I sensed moving in with him would feel more like we were a family and knowing we might be welcoming his baby daughter someday into our lives. She would need me, and I needed him.

One night as I was finishing moving most of my things, I called Joe to ask if he could help me move some of the heavier boxes to his house, and he bitterly replied he was busy with work as if I was inconveniencing him. "How am I supposed to move these?" He only responded by telling me to get the people I had worked with to do it. Was he testing me? I couldn't believe he wouldn't help me.

I called a friend of mine whose husband worked for the same broker I had worked for, and he was nice enough to come and move my heavy boxes. I felt embarrassed and had no excuse for Joe. I know he wasn't working at eight-thirty that evening. He was out with his work buddies having dinner and drinks and didn't want to be bothered. Moving in with him was just the beginning.

Chapter Three

Ex's and Oh's

Since I had lost my job, I was happy to answer phone calls for Joe for his tour business. He seemed to enjoy the relief of someone else taking care of the office work. It also allowed me time to pick up Ryan and Emma from school. I started answering phone calls every day, handling reservations for leisure and corporate bookings, and running his daily errands for him. Eventually, I was in charge of paying bills, submitting payroll for his employees, preparing his financial statements, and entering all of his bookkeeping. He liked to call me his operations manager.

His business slowly started to expand into other cities. I was his back-office support when he needed it. I never asked him for a salary of any kind, mainly because I was living in his house with my children, and he did help with my car payments, which I used for business. I stood by his side, offering moral support through his court dates with his ex-wife while he fought to get joint custody of Hannah, which was soon granted to him. Even though Christy wasn't awarded half of his business, the court documents stated he would have to pay child support, including back child support which totaled in the thousands. It became too much to bear, and I saw a side to him that I had never seen as he shouted at the top of his lungs— "Christy is a fu***** bitch and a loser!"

I was shocked at his vulgarity as his anger oozed from his eyes, which gave me a feeling of uneasiness.

"How could you say those things?"

"Do you realize she is only out to get my money? She is out to ruin me. She needs to move on and find someone else to screw over."

"How could you call her that? She's the mother of your child, even if you don't like her."

"You don't understand, Renee. You just don't get it."

He hurriedly walked past me, as the door to the garage slammed forcefully behind him. He stayed in the comfort of his *man cave* listening to his stereo for what seemed like hours. Luckily, Ryan and Emma were visiting with their father and didn't have to listen to his explosive outburst. It was only later, after going to bed that night, that I felt the weight of his body hitting the sheets. I somehow had to mentally prepare myself for the anger that I assumed would still be there the next day.

As I awoke to the morning sun peeking through the windows, I turned to see Joe still fast asleep. Pouring my cup of coffee, I heard the television in the bedroom go on. I brought his cup to him as I did every morning. He smiled as he told me that I treated him like a king. He casually got up, showered, dressed, and said he would see me later. Not once did he mention anything about Christy or her conniving ways. It was almost like what was said the night before had never happened.

Per court order, Christy was to bring Hannah over to the house and drop her off with him. He called me, making sure I was there because he wouldn't be home. He was busy, but he was always busy. Always on the go. I somehow didn't feel right intercepting Hannah at the door from his ex-wife that I had never met. However, he was insistent, stating that she could take him back to court if he wasn't at home when she dropped off Hannah at the designated time. How was that my fault? I felt he should have been there, if not by what was stated in court documents, then at least be there when his daughter showed up. But, I wanted to help. I adored Hannah and would, of course, be there.

Christy showed up at the front door giving me a once over as if I were the devil. I understood that it must have felt strange for her to see another woman in the house she had shared with Joe and now she was delivering her daughter to me. She was still bitter, and I could feel her tension and apprehensiveness on leaving Hannah with me. I promised her Joe would be home shortly, and as she turned to leave, she said, "You better be careful of Joe, especially if your children are living here too." I was shocked at her abrasiveness as she stood there waiting for my reaction.

I glanced down at Hannah. She had been standing by me at the door the whole time and had heard every word. She was only four and a half years old. Where was Joe? Why wasn't he here? I looked at Christy, and with as much confidence as I could muster, I said, "There's a time and a place for everything, and this is not the place and definitely not the time." There wasn't anything more to say as the door shut behind me.

Joe came home soon after and never once thought to say thank you. It was odd. I couldn't understand why he just expected me to do something that was so obviously important and meant so much to him and then act like it wasn't a big deal or even say thank you. I had told him what Christy had said and he laughed. "She's just jealous because you're prettier." He coolly strolled into the living room to watch television with Hannah. Discussion over.

More days like this followed. Christy dropping off Hannah and Joe not being there. She eventually started to warm up to me and could see that I cared about Hannah. One day she came to the door to pick up Hannah and invited me to a pool party. Why would she ask me to go? Something felt off. "Whose pool party is it?" I asked.

"It's Jenny's. You may know her. She dated Joe."

"Excuse me? You want me to go to a pool party with you to Joe's ex-girlfriend's house? Are you joking?"

"Actually, we are friends, and she's really nice. It will be fun, and Hannah likes going over there."

I knew what this was. I felt it. Christy was trying to get information from me to use against Joe somehow. My stomach was in knots as I politely declined and told her thanks, but no thanks. I couldn't help but wonder why she would befriend Joe's ex-girlfriend. Judging from what Joe had told me, I could only conclude that she wanted to use whatever piece of information she could get her hands on to use against him in court. When Christy took Joe to court yet again to dispute the back-child support and why it should be more, she mentioned that Joe was telling their daughter terrible things about her. She was making him out to be a bad parent, and Joe was angry almost daily over that time.

One evening after dinner, he gave me a beautiful pair of diamond earrings and told me to put them on because I needed something on my ears. I had never really worn much jewelry but thought it was very sweet, and even facing Christy in court with the weight of the world on his shoulders, he had thought of me. He thanked me for standing by him with everything he was going through and then just as quickly, said, "I'll never get married again though."

Was that his way of making sure I knew this important piece of information? I guess in some ways, after being married for twelve years, I really didn't want to go through another marriage again anytime soon, so I brushed off what

25

he had said, thinking he was just hurt by what Christy was doing to him. So, he didn't want to get married again. But would I?

Chapter Four

The Love Bomber

What I didn't know at the time was Joe was using a tactic called "*Love bombing*" on me. He overwhelmed my normal sense of caution with his charm, charisma, and passion. I was on cloud nine and felt like I was his whole world. All of the oddities that the intuitive part of myself had encountered in the last few months quickly disappeared. He loved me. He needed me. He couldn't live without me. These were the words he would use frequently to reel me in even deeper into his world. I didn't know what a sociopath was then and that I was living among one.

I was so overwhelmed by his love and attention that I didn't even stop to think about his bizarre behavior lately. I was being lavished with compliments and his over-the-top charm. Love bombing, unlike real love, is a sociopath's goal of acquiring someone because it boosts their ego. I was no different than a shiny new toy that captured his attention for the moment. It simply was all an illusion. That charismatic exterior that Joe used so effectively on me was one of manipulation with a lack of conscience and genuine emotion. He had me—hook, line, and sinker.

Life was good at the moment. Then, as if he had flipped a switch, he started acting indifferent and angry at me for no reason at all, and I started wondering if I was doing something wrong. At the drop of a dime, Joe would go from acting like he wanted nothing to do with me, then making me feel sorry for him, to the point of even feeling like I needed to prove myself to him. The red flags were obviously there; however, I chose to ignore them every time. But he loved me. He even said so. The times he pushed me away, I would be showered with his attention and affection once more. Sometimes this happened within days, other times within hours of what can only be described as a Dr. Jekyll and Mr. Hyde personality.

I knew he was going through a lot with Christy and eventually would have to go through hell trying to get custody of his daughter in Texas that would soon be born. This weighed heavily on me. Many times, I wasn't sure if I was ready to be a mother all over again, especially to someone else's child that was so young. We went to counseling over it and spoke freely about what we both faced with a new addition to our blended family. It meant a lot of changes.

As I tried to curl up next to him in bed one night, he seemed put off that I would even touch him. "You sure are needy. What's wrong with you?" I quickly turned away.

Where had that come from? Why would he say something so mean? I just wanted to be close to him, and I couldn't help but think, did I really come across as needy? Even though I was bothered by his choice of words, I never mentioned it the next day. He was up and out the door. Busy, busy, busy. I spent my days running his business from our home office. There were no days off. Calls were transferred to my cell phone from the business line so I wouldn't miss booking a reservation. Maybe I just wanted a word of encouragement since each day was filled with bits and pieces of negativity. You never knew what mood and mindset would greet you when he walked in the door.

I believe my children detected that something was off about Joe even earlier then I realized. It was only years later after I left him that Emma mentioned she had felt uncomfortable when she first met Joe, and there was something about him that she just didn't like. He had intimidated her from the very beginning. I never even knew this. It made me feel awful inside. Knowing that my child was fearful.

Ryan looked up to him as the man of the house and just wanted his approval. Since Joe operated a tour company, Ryan wanted to follow in his footsteps and looked at him as a mentor. Joe promised Ryan that he would train him and show him the ins and outs of the business if he worked for him as an employee. Almost a teenager now, Ryan was excited about this opportunity and that Joe was using his own personal time to train him.

On many occasions, however, Ryan would go to work with Joe, then come home with an angry look on his face and go straight to his room. Joe would be trailing right behind him while yelling at the top of his lungs that Ryan needed to learn to listen. His anger was evident by his posture and tone as he continued to raise his voice to make sure everyone heard him. I was disturbed by his wild outbursts and immature tangents, but my fear held me back from confronting him about it.

An argument would ensue if I did. I wanted it to stop but became paralyzed by his words. Yet, another red flag that waved wildly to get my attention but failed. It was sad to think that the man I originally viewed as my knight in shining armor, my prince charming, had devolved into a hostile, domineering, and parasitic villain.

Chapter Five

Daddy's Boy

It was now June, and I was alone in the house with Joe on Father's Day. Ryan and Emma had gone to spend it with their father, and Christy was dropping off Hannah mid-morning. We were planning to meet Joe's father, Nick, for a Father's Day brunch. I called my father who lived in North Carolina to wish him a wonderful day. It was hard not seeing him much, but I hadn't seen him through most of my childhood years.

My mother and father were divorced when I was just six years old, and she wanted to stay in Arizona while he moved back to North Carolina. I grew up believing he had a family of his own and wanted nothing to do with me, but when I was old enough, my curiosity got the best of me. I had to know for myself. Searching for someone back then proved to be more difficult, but once we re-connected, I knew we would be in each other's lives forever. As a child, losing touch with a parent has an impact on your soul, especially not having a parent around through those important adolescent years. Maybe that is partially why I was drawn to Joe in the first place. We understood what it was like growing up without the other parent.

I was happy to meet Nick for the first time that day. We had a reservation at Wright's restaurant at the Biltmore hotel. It was a popular spot among tourists with an ambiance that was perfect for the holiday. Joe and I were enjoying our mimosas on the patio when Nick walked in. I knew it was his father before he even approached us as he had similar features with silver hair. Hannah ran over to hug him as he glanced in my direction. Locking eyes, I offered him a friendly smile.

"Hello, Nick, it's nice to meet you." He gave me a quick nod with a smile as we made our way to our table. Sitting across from me, his eyes narrowed as he took me in. I looked over at Joe as he leaned back in his chair, expressionless. Judging from Nick's weathered face, I could tell that time had taken its toll. Joe had once told me that his father grew up in Tennessee and was in the Navy.

Sitting there, while eating the delicious food, the focus of discussion was on Hannah, followed by a moment of awkward silence. I felt like they were both waiting for me to say something, so I asked Nick about growing up on a farm in Tennessee and what his days were like in the Navy, as my father had also served in the Navy. Nick was surprisingly forthcoming and started to share some of his personal stories from his younger days.

After listening to his stories and the hardships he endured, it became apparent what a lifetime of victories and failures can do to a person. I wished him happy Father's Day as we left, and felt it was nice getting to know the man that raised Joe himself. I told Joe that as well.

He gave me a peculiar look and said, "I didn't even know those things about my father. He's never talked about his life like that."

I was surprised. "Did you ever ask your father about his life?"

"No, but he never liked talking about his past and growing up."

I couldn't believe that no one had ever asked him, and here I just thought to ask only the small details I knew about him and he openly shared that part of his life with me. I felt good at that moment. It was a good day.

His father would make appearances at the house now and then, and I could tell that Joe looked up to him for his approval. More and more, it seemed that every time he was conflicted about what to do, he would call Nick or tell me that he had to call his father and ask him what he should do. What should he do about Christy? How was he going to pay her the back-child support in a lump sum? What should he do about his other daughter that would soon be born? If he had questions about his business or employees, insurance, health care, or just about anything, I heard—"I have to ask my dad."

I understood needing another opinion, but he always did what his father would say. He was a thirty-nine-year-old man that still needed his father's approval to where it became almost obsessive. I was starting to think that he was under his father's control. I knew they were close because Joe had grown up without his mother. I felt sorry for him. I sympathized with him, and not having my father around for so many years, I related to him.

I needed him and he needed me. We were two pieces of a puzzle that fit. It would be okay. I would be there for him, but his father was the only one he would listen to. When he had too much on his plate and something didn't go his way, he would unleash his rage without any remorse after the fact. Joe started acting indifferent when he would go to work, only to leave me wondering if he was coming home for dinner.

I made dinner every night the children were with us since there were days filled with homework, studying, soccer, and horseback riding lessons at a local equestrian center. I knew that Joe needed his "guy time" with his friends, which were the people he worked with. I was never invited to these get-togethers, but I was content at home with the children until he started staying out more and more. At times I expected him home for dinner, I would text him and he would tell me he was on his way and then not come home until three hours later, always having an excuse as to why he had to stay out.

He explained how he couldn't just come home. There were discussions about work, and it would have been rude of him to leave. Busy, busy, busy. Over and over again, I heard, *"I'm on my way."* If I had done the same thing to him, I know I would have not heard the end of it. It seemed that there was a different set of rules that applied to him. The sad thing was when his daughter Hannah was with us, he wouldn't even show up to spend time with her in the evenings or tuck her in bed to say good night. She would continue to ask me, "Why isn't my daddy home?" It broke my heart. I tried to tell him that she would ask for him, but he always had an excuse and brushed it off like he spent plenty of time with her. It was disheartening.

When his father was over however, it amazed me that he could still ridicule me or the kids right in front of him. Nick, of course. always sided with Joe, but there were a few occasions where he stood up for me and quieted Joe down. Once, when we were eating out on the patio of a local restaurant, Joe suddenly burst out that he didn't like the fact that I had found another job and told me that nothing was being done at home. He had to watch the kids and cook at times, help with homework, and do laundry, which he never did much of. He said this out loud for everyone sitting around us to hear.

My face became flushed in anger from being ridiculed in public. I tried to speak to defend myself, and Joe quickly cut me off, continuing to do so, not letting me reply. Nick quickly jumped in and yelled, "Joe, you need to hear her out. Let her speak." Was his father defending me? I liked to think he was. I could see the angry scowl on Joe's face start to disappear. His father had such power over him.

Not only had he embarrassed me in public and in front of his father, but he had also chastised me about my new job when in the beginning he had been supportive of me getting it. With my voice quivering, I managed to say, "I'll only be working part-time, and I will still be home to answer office calls and take care of the kids." Why couldn't he be supportive of my goals when all I was doing was supporting his? It seemed unfair.

He knew that I was visibly shaken by his words and only managed to let out a sigh as if it didn't matter. We drove home in silence. I was hoping for an apology but never received it as Joe never apologized for anything. No words were spoken between us as we laid in bed that night. As he turned on the television, I thought again about dinner with his father that evening and suddenly, it hit me—Joe was a "Daddy's Boy."

Chapter Six

The Con Artist

Joe enjoyed demeaning me and he didn't feel bad about it at all. He made me feel so guilty when I spent time with the few friends I had left that I started to give excuses on why I couldn't join them or make plans. I couldn't understand why he would become so cross, even when I attended a friend's baby shower. He was so convincing; I couldn't even see that I was being controlled and manipulated. It was all about him and what he wanted—and he didn't want me around anyone else. I was not allowed to have an opinion of my own; for if I did, he would lash out at me.

He took me into his confidence, whereas I started doubting myself and trusting him. Within months of living together, I felt lost, confused, alienated from my friends and family, and unimportant. I felt more like the hired help than a partner. Something in me started to change. I was losing myself, the fun-loving part of myself that I knew. My energy had been replaced with a toxicity, slowly poisoning my heart and mind. The man who said he loved me and would do anything to see me happy was manipulative, aggressive, and deceiving. Yet, still, I stayed. He was a con artist—and a good one.

Within a month, due to his relentless negative comments and guilt-ridden words, I ended up quitting the part-time office job and once again dedicated myself full time to his business. I now became dependent financially on him, and in retrospect, I believe he didn't want me to earn my own income so that I remained completely under his power and control. He had temporarily hired his friend's girlfriend to help with bookkeeping and filing, but whenever I left the house, it always felt strangely odd seeing the two of them in his office laughing and carrying on about something that had happened at work.

They had known each other for years from previously working together, but I always had an uneasy feeling around the two of them as the thought crossed my mind that they might have gotten together at one time. It was a gut feeling, which I, of course, ignored. I had asked him once if they had ever dated, and his response was cold, as he muttered, "You're crazy." I noticed that he never answered me directly. Joe had a way of avoiding direct questions and going around topics, making you feel as if you were indeed, crazy.

Since I took care of submitting payroll, I often spoke to some of his employees. I had been told on several occasions that Joe's company was thriving because of everything I did for him. I knew how hard I worked for him, and I know he knew it too as Joe had once told me that no other woman had done more for him than me. Ron, an employee that had been with him for years, knew Joe's dark side, and once said, "Joe would be eight feet under if it wasn't for you." That felt good to hear, but I wanted his company to grow and to succeed, and it was.

Even the web designer who maintained his company's website had told me that she knew who ran the business, and it only validated what I already knew, but it also felt wonderful knowing that others knew this too. Joe had a lot of baggage when I met him and even more so when he told me about Desiree having his child. Being in a relationship with him meant that I had to endure all of that baggage too, but it never seemed to end with both Christy and Desiree trying to make life miserable for him. The obsessive phone calls and texts started from Desiree about him flying out to Texas so he could be there when their baby was born. He wanted nothing to do with being there or with her.

He had even tried convincing her in the early stages of the pregnancy to get an abortion. She, of course, refused. It made me question why he would want to get custody of the child if he didn't want her at all or wasn't excited to be a father. My heart went out to that baby that was days away from being born. I tried to keep my distance and not respond to much of his emotional outbursts, but sometimes it proved difficult to do since he would insult me or my children, who were like targets to him. They could never do anything right in his eyes. We had two little dachshunds that liked to wander off, and we always made sure the gate in the backyard stayed closed so they wouldn't get out. They were good little escape artists. One day, Joe had left the gate open and I could see it was unlatched, so I asked Ryan to go and close it.

Being the typical preteen, he rolled his eyes and went to close it. Joe had witnessed the eye-rolling, and that's all it took for him to go off into a violent rage. He started to yell so loudly that I couldn't help but think that the neighbors could hear. He was constantly putting Ryan down and this time was no different. "Why do you have such a fu***** attitude? If you don't shape up, you'll never amount to fu***** anything in life! You don't want to be a loser, do you? Rolling your eyes is unacceptable, and I won't put up with it!"

Ryan just stood there motionless as if he was exhausted from hearing Joe's foul mouth and bizarre behavior. I tried to calm him down and to tell him it was fine, and Ryan had closed the gate as I asked. This angered Joe even more. He turned on me then, "Why are you always defending him? He needs to know that's not fu***** acceptable! He's going to grow up like a spoiled brat if we don't lay down some ground rules."

Something in me then snapped. A defense mechanism perhaps, but I felt like the mother lion protecting her cubs from a predator and couldn't help but say, "How dare you lecture me about my children when you flat out told me you didn't even graduate high school and snuck out of your dad's house on many occasions! Oh, and don't forget that Hannah just smacked you across the face earlier when she didn't want to clean up her room! Maybe she should be on time-out for that as that's not acceptable behavior either!"

Oh, I had done it! It felt good to say my peace and defend Ryan, but Joe was mortified that I had stood my ground and challenged his authority as a parent, not to mention his wild outburst. Striking the air with his fists, he burst into Emma's room next, pulling out her clothes from the closet and throwing them on the floor in a pile. "You, little missy, better hang all of these clothes back up in an orderly fashion. Your closet is a mess and quit looking at me like that!"

Emma was almost crying, sitting on the floor in her room wondering what she had done. He had only attacked her to hurt me. Emma was the cleanest person in the house. She always made her bed and kept her room clean, so for Joe to attack her in this manner was ridiculous. I started to cry, and he then he grabbed Hannah's hand and said they were leaving. Hannah was even crying. We had planned to take the children to the Oasis water park that day. I told him it wasn't fair, and he needed to apologize to Ryan and Emma for his behavior and using foul language.

He refused and told me that I needed to get a handle on my children and left. He still took Hannah to the water park that day. It made me sick. I had knots in my stomach and felt the anxiety creeping in. I apologized to Ryan and

Emma and had no excuse for his behavior. I almost left him that day, and I probably would have had I had a place to go. I worked for him and didn't have a source of income. I knew my ex-husband couldn't take Ryan and Emma as he worked so much and traveled. I was too embarrassed to ask anyone for help. Help from what?

My friends and family thought he was a great guy who loved me so much. Joe even had my father believing it. How did I explain all of his bizarre behavior? What was I going to do? How was Joe going to act when he came home later that evening? It was hard for me to get my mind around his madness. I knew in my bones that not a single, normal, and rational woman alive could have felt safe, secure, and happy under the circumstances I was living in. His outlandish claims and assertions followed by his constant outbursts of anger had me questioning my sanity.

Chapter Seven
Secrets and Lies

After that horrific encounter and not even a trace of an apology, I never looked at Joe the same way again. I received the silent treatment for the next few days, and his episodes of rage had not been questioned. It was his way to manipulate me and condition me to not ever question him again. I wasn't sure what was wrong with him but knew it wasn't normal, even with the amount of stress he had been under lately.

He started openly flirting with other women in front of me, telling one that she was so beautiful on what was supposed to have been a dinner out together, on his suggestion, not mine. Later, I had told him that wasn't appropriate and of course wanted to know why he would do that. His response was one of, "You're just jealous," "You're crazy," or even, "I was just kidding around." I had been disrespected and blamed for everything so often that I had come to expect the worst, and he delivered it every time. He would do this on many occasions as if he had something to prove.

We even went out one night to a wine bar to enjoy some wine tasting, only he started chatting with a cute blonde sitting behind us about her friend that sang there, which led to him getting her phone number so she could let him know where her friend was playing next. It was obvious by their playful smiles and body language, that they were flirting. I was sitting right there the whole time, silently crying out in anger.

I was a catch, I was pretty, I was funny, I was intelligent, a good mother, and a compassionate and caring person. This went through my mind as I watched him flirt with her. I would have never done that to him, but oh, how I wanted him to know what it felt like to be so disrespected and tossed aside. I couldn't control the hurt I felt watching the two of them as I suddenly stood up to leave. "I'll be waiting outside for you once you're done." That hit him apparently because he came outside right away and said, "We were just talking."

"Did you get her number?"

"Yes, in fact, I did, but it's only to talk about the next location her friend would be playing at so we can go."

"What? You could care less about the singer. It's written all over your face, Joe. I'm not stupid."

"I don't know what you're talking about! You're crazy!"

I couldn't make sense of why he would have flirted with another woman right in front of me, and all I could think was—

here we go again. Later that night, once he fell asleep, I reached into his jacket pocket and found the piece of paper with her name and phone number. I ripped it up and threw it in the trash. Good riddance! Why did I have to convince him that I was all that he needed? People would say how lucky he was to have someone like me in his life. Didn't he believe that? I was so confused by it all and yet, so entangled in what would become his web of lies. I had an uneasy feeling that something was wrong with this relationship, and yet, I just brushed it aside and remained quiet.

Right when I would feel at my lowest point and question why I was with him, I was swept up in his empty promises, romantic pursuits, and all his BS about true love and being his soulmate. He would say anything to make me fall for him all over again. He could make my heart flutter and then crush it just as quickly. In retrospect, he didn't love me, as sociopaths do not know love. I was only rewarded with what he called love if I was happy and indulged *his* desires.

On a day he took off from work, his longtime friend Jack came to visit from Las Vegas. They had known each other for fifteen years and didn't let the distance between them keep them from the brotherly connection they shared. They had been through a lot together and liked reminiscing about the old days. Jack had brought his sister, Tanya, with him on this trip. She was kind and soft-spoken, and I enjoyed hearing stories of the times they shared. We were all having drinks outside on the patio when Jack had mentioned a party they had back in the day, and out of the blue, he blurted out, "Yeah, Joe, don't you remember getting together with my sister? You guys did it right in her room."

I almost spit out my drink as I looked at Tanya, and asked her, "You were with Joe?" Her face flushed, and she looked at Joe for an answer, not knowing how to respond. Tanya was a heavyset girl with a plain-Jane kind of look and didn't seem like the type of woman Joe would be attracted to. Judging from what I had witnessed firsthand, he was only drawn to women that were physically fit and attractive.

I couldn't comprehend why Jack chose to bring such a private matter up, except maybe for the shock value or maybe to view all of our reactions. The topic had become very inappropriate and I squirmed in my chair. "We weren't having sex," Joe replied with a laugh. "She was reading scripture to me."

I almost peed my pants. This man listening to someone read scripture to him? I knew he was lying. Somehow, the subject was quickly changed. It only made me think, *what else is he hiding from me?* My life with Joe after that was filled with many secrets and lies. I was a pawn in his game of life, and it was all for control and power. He created a world of insecurity, fear, and isolation to make me think that I needed him, and I couldn't make it without him. Trying to prove his lies as the truth became the price of my reality and psychological health.

Chapter Eight

Oh Baby!

With the arrival of Joe's daughter, Callie, I felt more of a need to be there. He hadn't been there for her birth and Desiree and her parents were continually trying to convince him to fly out and meet his daughter. They sent photos of her birth. She was a beautiful baby with jet black hair and dark brown eyes. He had told me he was conflicted with flying out there as he felt that her family would gang up on him to try and convince him to be part of Callie's life there in Texas.

Desiree's parents had temporary custody of Callie until further notice. A fight to gain custody of Callie was now on his radar. Desiree only saw me as an obstacle, and I was in the way between her and Joe. I started to receive numerous threats on the business line and listened to the vulgar words coming from her mouth. She attempted to humiliate me on social media, going as far as calling me a whore. Why was she attacking me?

The reality of her calling me a whore was quite comedic as she was the one who had gotten pregnant and had a baby out of wedlock. It was only a year later that we found out she was pregnant again by another man who lived in Texas. I felt sorry for any child that had to endure being raised by a drug abuser as a mother.

She was jealous of the relationship and wanted Joe to somehow be with her so they could be together as a family. I had told Joe about her slandering me all over social media and he just laughed. Was this funny to him somehow? Here was a man I had stood up for and defended, yet he couldn't even defend me to a woman he didn't want anything to do with? A woman he barely knew that sometimes lived on the streets to supply her drug habit. This was all his fault, and yet, I had to experience the repercussions with him.

I then asked him point-blank if I was in the way and if he wanted to try to have a life with Desiree. It hurt asking, but I needed to know. He responded with a "No, I don't want to be with Desiree. I don't love her. She was just a fling. Having a child with her doesn't mean I want to be with her. I love you! You're the one I want to share my life with." Hmm, I wondered what had happened to the man that had said he didn't want to bring a child into the world knowing that he didn't marry her mother, however, I didn't ask him.

When Callie was just three months old, he decided to go and see her and asked me to go with him. At first, I didn't want to but thought I needed to be strong for him as he didn't want to face Desiree's family alone. We walked into Desiree's parent's house and were greeted by Desiree herself, along with her sister, mother, and father. It was the most awkward and uncomfortable feeling as everyone was surprised to see me there. Joe had obviously not told them I would be coming with him. I could feel the anger building up in Desiree. She could have shot daggers through her eyes at me, but her parents were very polite.

Trying to avoid her stare, I watched Joe as they placed Callie in his arms. It was a tender moment. My heart went out to that baby as she wrapped her tiny hand around his finger. It was the sweetest sight. I'm sure my presence there was unsettling for everyone, especially Desiree. She refused to accept that Joe wasn't there to work things out with her as she walked straight out the front door and never returned.

Startled, Joe asked, "Did she leave?" Desiree's mother only replied, "Yes, this is hard for her." I knew what she meant. It was difficult enough seeing Joe walk in to hold their baby for the first time, but it was even harder because I was there. I was the elephant in the room, and all eyes were on me. I felt I shouldn't be there. I just wanted to be back home with my children.

Joe didn't want to fight for custody of Callie while she was still so young and decided to wait until she turned a year old. Even though he had made some effort to make periodic visits, the courts viewed him as an absentee father that had abandoned his child from birth, so he continued to make regular visits to Texas to see Callie until the next court date and all the ones that followed thereafter. I ended up staying at home on most of his visits as I still had to take care of Ryan and Emma, and Hannah when she was with us.

By then, Joe's ex-wife, Christy, knew of Callie and trusted me to be there for Hannah when Joe traveled. She was cordial to me at Hannah's school plays and soccer games. Emma and Hannah had become very close, and Emma would even sometimes go over to Christy's house to have a sleepover with Hannah. It was sweet to see the two of them getting along so well. It warmed my heart. All of my attention was on them and running the company.

The family court wanted to see that Joe was making regular visits and that Callie was comfortable being with him. Desiree's mother and father continued to raise her until a decision was reached by the court. Desiree, however, would disappear for days at a time with no contact, and Joe made sure the court was aware it was unsafe to leave their daughter with Desiree unsupervised, due to her history with drugs.

For now, we just had to wait and see what the outcome would be and how the judge in the case would rule on Callie's fate. There were times when Joe would come home showering me with gifts, maybe thinking it was too much for me to grasp. Through all of the travel, stress, and emotional havoc it played in our lives, I really didn't feel bad for Joe; however, I did for Callie, who so badly needed

a mother. I wanted to protect her from the world and I
didn't even know her. It was a nurturing instinct that any
loving mother could relate to.

Chapter Nine

What Doesn't Kill You

Joe was a good provider and appeared at times to be very giving; however, it was with an agenda as he knew he could always bring it up and throw it in my face at a later time. Even with the diamond earrings he had surprised me with, he would ask why I wasn't wearing them one day and make me feel as if I was unappreciative, such as, "Do you know how much those earrings cost? They weren't cheap and I went out of my way to buy them for you. You won't even wear them? What, you don't like them?"

I honestly would have preferred that he never purchased them because I was constantly reminded how much they cost. Everything was about the money for Joe. Money, of course, is important to survive, and I understood his motivation and how hard we both worked to keep his business running, but it's all I would hear about every single day.

I was exhausted from his childish temper tantrums when he didn't get his way or when he was having a bad day, which was pretty often. Sometimes, his episodes of rage didn't even feel like it was seeded in real anger. It was a way he could manipulate me, and he knew it. I slowly started to become immune to his angry outbursts and stopped fighting back at times as I knew I would never win. We would never have a difference of opinion unless I wanted to hear him scream at the top of his lungs. Many times, I just agreed with what he wanted or had to say to avoid his incurring wrath.

On one particular day, I could tell that he was already in a mood as he was running late to meet his tour group. People started to call in asking where he was, and I apologized to them but before I could tell them anything else, he said, "Tell them I had a flat tire and will be there shortly." He had a stack of mail in his hand that he needed to get to the post office and somehow, this set off his anger. Once I hung up the phone, he realized he was running even later because he still had to go to the post office. He knew I would go there for him, but I believe he wanted me to feel sorry for him. "I can take the mail for you, Joe. Just go meet your tour group." In what I can only call a fit of rage, he threw the stack of mail all over the kitchen floor. "Fine! Take it! Now, I'm going to be fu***** later than I thought!"

I'm not sure what had set him off. I was only trying to help. He was yelling and carrying on and wasting even more time by throwing his wild tantrum. At this point, I had enough. "What do you want me to do? Cancel your tour group?" He didn't answer. I suddenly felt uncomfortable as if I was going to be verbally attacked in some manner. The phone rang again. His employees were standing by asking where he was. "Joe, I will just tell them you're going to cancel the tour today. It's already forty-five minutes past the meeting time."

Staring me down, I saw nothing but a shell of a person in his eyes as he muttered under his breath, "If you cancel the ride, I'll kill you." I was shocked! I had never heard him say he would kill me. A part of me was terrified while the other part of me thought he was just threatening me, as he always did. Of course, had I really thought he would physically hurt me or act on his words, I would have run out of the house and not looked back.

With my voice quivering and still quite shaken, I told his employees that he would be there shortly. He stormed off, screaming vulgarities as he drove away. I felt numb and completely helpless. What had just happened? Had the neighbors heard? My anxiety was at an all-time high. Why does this man hate me? It was how I felt at the moment. I sat down and cried. I picked the mail up off the floor and drove it to the post office as I had said I would. I really didn't want to after what he had said and the way he had acted, but I knew it would cause more harm if I didn't.

I could only think that this man loved to see me suffer. Later that evening, he tried repeatedly calling me. I didn't answer. I was angry and hurt and didn't want to hear his excuses, his voice, or any more of his evil rants. I needed to breathe. I wanted him to go away for a while and allow me to recover from the pain he had inflicted on me. I started drinking excessively. It numbed the pain and the hurt that weighed heavily on me, even for the short amount of time, it offered relief. It started with drinking a glass of wine, then two, then eventually the whole bottle.

The wine was just the beginning to many nights being at home alone after the kids had gone to bed. While he was out at *dinner* almost every night until midnight, I drank anything available to me. Rum, gin, vodka, and wine. I became dependent on the relief it offered me. The person I knew myself to be was buried and gone and replaced by someone else I didn't even recognize. What had I become?

I was nothing more than his doormat. He wiped his feet on me and made me feel like dirt. Still, I stayed. I was completely under his control. If only he could see how good I was for him, he would change and be that loving man he had been in the beginning to me. Yes, I believed that. I couldn't see what was now so obvious, but I didn't know what a sociopath was then. Why couldn't have someone told me?

Joe had apologized to me for his chaotic episode, and I, of course not wanting him to start yet another fight with me, accepted his apology. He blamed it on all of the stress he was going through with trying to obtain custody of Callie. It was only a few weeks later when he was at it again, although this time he was on the phone with me, complaining that his life was nothing and everything he was going through was just too much. I tried consoling him, even telling him everything would work out. He just needed to remain strong, have faith, and give it time. Getting sole custody of Callie wasn't going to happen overnight.

He started talking about wanting to end his life, which at the time I took seriously. On the phone that day with him, I became scared. "I'm saying goodbye to you, Renee, and I won't be coming back. I can't take it anymore. It's too much. I just want to tell you that I love you. Tell Hannah that I love her." I was terrified. Was he really going to kill himself? Where was he? Things didn't seem that bad that he had to end his life.

I didn't think at the time that he was just playing me. I didn't know better and I sure didn't want to live with the guilt if he did kill himself and I hadn't done anything to try and stop him. I tried consoling him, but he just hung up. I immediately called him back but he wouldn't answer. What do I do? I had to do something. The only thing that came to mind was to call his father. I knew he would listen to Nick; so with what courage I had left, I called him.

Luckily, Nick answered. Sobbing anxiously, I told him what Joe had said. He started to laugh and said, "Renee, it will be okay. Joe will be fine. He isn't going to hurt himself. I'll call him and then call you back. Don't worry." It surprised me how confident Nick was knowing that his son wouldn't do anything to hurt himself. After a few minutes passed, the phone rang. Nick reassured me that Joe was fine and was coming home. Everything was okay.

In her book, "Red Flags of Love Fraud: 10 Signs Your Dating A Sociopath[2]," author Donna Andersen conducted an internet survey of people who believed they were romantically involved with a sociopath. A total of 1,352 people completed the survey. Twenty-one percent of respondents said the sociopath they were involved with threatened to commit suicide, or actually went through with the act.

Why does a sociopath threaten suicide? It's not about their feelings of pain or an act of desperation. It all comes down to control. Joe knew he could manipulate me and win. He wanted me to feel guilt-ridden and sorry for him, which worked, and I believed he would do it again.

I was relieved he hadn't hurt himself but now scared that he would be angry with me for calling his father. Who would be walking through that door? I waited fearfully for his return. I heard his truck pull into the driveway; my heart feeling as if it was in my stomach. Joe walked through the door with a look of disgust on his face as if I had exposed his perfect performance. His voice was hoarse as if he'd been yelling for hours. "How could you call my father and tell him I was going to kill myself?"

"Are you joking, Joe? Do you want to know why I called your father? Because he's the only one you will listen to and I knew he would be the only one to stop you if you were serious about ending it all. I don't want that on my conscience, and if you had gone through with it, at least I would have known I didn't just stand by and do nothing to help. I don't want you hurt and I love you, that's why!" I realized then that my voice had escalated, angry at him for allowing me to worry about taking his life and not knowing if he would go through with it.

Que the silent treatment. He ignored me as if I wasn't there, still angry that I had called his father. He knew I cared and loved him enough to take some kind of action. He was enjoying this mind game. He made the rules, and he played to win.

Chapter Ten

Gaslit

By then, Joe's controlling and manipulating ways overrode my reality. He had been gaslighting me from the very beginning of our relationship, but now I found myself confused and always apologizing. At times, he would even get angry at me for apologizing, which was only because he wanted to argue, and the apology would shut him down. I made excuses for his behavior and for myself at times, believing I was crazy to stay in the relationship. Why did I feel like I needed him? Even worse, why did I feel I would never find love again if I left?

I was isolated from my friends and family. Any friends I had left had now given up on inviting me to any get-togethers because I always had a reason I couldn't go, which was really Joe making me feel guilty if I did. I would see my mother and sister every now and then for special occasions, but beyond that, Joe had exhausted me to the point where I was unable to even defend myself.

I recently came across an article by bestselling author, Shahida Arabi, "7 Gaslighting Phrases Malignant Narcissists, Sociopaths, and Psychopaths Use To Silence You.[3]" Sadly, Joe had used every one of these seven gaslighting phrases on me. I've included them here.

1. You're crazy/you have mental health issues/you need help.

2. You're just insecure and jealous.

3. You're too sensitive/you're overreacting.

4. It was just a joke. You have no sense of humor.

5. You need to let it go. Why are you bringing this up?

6. You're the problem here, not me.

7. I never said or did that. You're imagining things.

I believe Joe liked manipulating me because it was how he learned to negotiate in his world and get what he wanted. I noticed that the stories he would tell me about work and being out late wouldn't add up at times, in turn, which meant he was lying to me. What was he hiding? He would never waver or admit he was lying even if I tried telling him that his story had inconsistencies from the time he told it before. He would, of course, use of one of the gaslighting phrases mentioned, such as, "I never said that."

He was so caught up in his lies that the distinction between truth and fiction became blurred. If I didn't buy his story, he would take it a step further and try to play the victim, usually with a story about Christy or Desiree and what they had done to him, trying to gain my sympathy, to the point I would doubt my own mind. If I became angry with him about being lied to, he would then attack me for not caring enough about him or not caring about the problem that he was playing victim about. He was distracting me from the real truth of what he was dishonestly doing.

I began doubting things and second-guessing what I wanted and who I was. I started to become suspicious of his lies, and paranoia overwhelmed me to point that I started to wonder if I was going crazy. My self-doubt slowly caused me to question my reality. I was *"Gaslit."* I became discouraged and fearful and even started to question other people's motives.

Joe kept his power and control this way. He wouldn't lose and would reject criticism of any kind. I noticed he would only stop if I became silent and chose to ignore him, which sometimes would be so difficult, secretly wanting to stand up and defend myself against his hurtful words, his lies, and exaggerations. Soon after, Joe mentioned that he had to go on a business trip for work, and of all places, to Texas. He would be gone for two weeks while he met with some of the manufacturing engineers that he frequently did business with. It was an opportunity to meet with them in person and go over new ideas for the equipment he used for his tours. He also told me he would be taking a trip to San Antonio to visit with Callie over that time.

I didn't think anything more about it and honestly, it would be a welcome relief to have some distance from him. I wanted that tightness in my chest to go away, to breathe normally again. I wondered, would he miss me? Perhaps he was really going there to be in someone else's company. I couldn't help but think the worst. After all, he had met Desiree there. The way I had been feeling lately made me doubt his words and his trust. Little did I know, I was right.

Chapter Eleven

The Betrayal

Over the time Joe was gone, I kept myself busy with booking reservations, and the daily activities with the children around school, homework, and soccer games. Joe would call me most days, but there were a few days in between that I never heard from him. I had come to expect this by now, so it became my normal. If I tried calling him, he was always too busy to talk or in a rush to get off the phone. Busy, busy, busy.

At Hannah's soccer games, Emma, Ryan, and I became her cheering section. Christy was always at her games, but on this day, she came over and sat down next to us and said hello. I became distinctly aware of the direction the conversation was headed. "Have you heard anything about the custody hearing?" Callie was now three years old, and after the many court hearings and enforcements, a final hearing had been set with the family court to determine custody the following month. Whether Callie remained with her grandparents or if Joe was awarded sole custody, Callie's life would soon change forever.

I wasn't comfortable talking about our personal life with Christy unless it involved Hannah. Knowing what she had said in the past about Joe and our relationship, nothing said around her was off-limits from spreading like wildfire. My reply was short. "Nothing to report yet." I felt if Joe had wanted Christy to know, then he would have told her. What she said next was something I never thought I would hear her say. "Well, Joe better not screw things up with you." All I could do was shyly smile in return.

That weekend, Joe arrived home exhausted from his trip. He had a tour group scheduled that day, and he wanted to nap for a few hours before he had to meet everyone. He handed me his phone as he greeted me with a hug. "Can you make sure you contact Adrian and tell him what time we'll be meeting?" Adrian was one of his new employees and was still learning the business.

"Sure, no worries. I'll text him in a bit when I'm at the stables with Emma." As Emma was turning out her horse in the arena, I retrieved Joe's phone from my pocket. I looked for the name Adrian in his contacts and my eyes fell on a name I didn't recognize—Adriane. I could see there were many text messages sent over the last week, and as my eyes started to scan over the words, a feeling of sickening anguish washed over me. My legs felt like cement, and I couldn't move. I wanted to vomit.

Joe had been texting this Adriane person since the beginning of his trip. From what I could gather, he had met her at one of the meetings he attended. He went on to ask her to the local casino there and wanted to have dinner and drinks with her. Then, he offered to teach her the business. I knew they had spent some time together based on the numerous text messages. He went on to tell her how beautiful she was, how he felt such a connection to her and would love to come back to Texas to *train* her. If that wasn't bad enough, she mentioned she had to ask her father if it was okay for Joe to come out to Texas to *train* her. Her father? How old was this girl? The sickening feeling in my stomach worsened.

My biggest fear had come to life before my eyes. Emma ran over to me with a look of concern. "Mom, are you okay? You're shaking." I looked at her, trying to gather my thoughts of what I had just read. "I'm fine." I couldn't bear the thought of telling her what Joe had done as she was still young and this was between Joe and me. Somehow, I managed to get to my car, drive to Panera Bread for a sandwich I promised her, and drove home.

I told Emma to go outside and play with the dogs as I didn't want her to hear what was about to take place. Joe had woken up from the sound of the door slamming as I walked into the bedroom. I tossed the bag with his sandwich I had brought him as it hit him in the chest. He looked at me with a startled expression on his face. "What did you do that for?"

"I should ask you the same question, Joe."

"What are you talking about?"

"This is what I'm talking about," as I threw his phone at him, displaying the open text messages to Adriane. His face went ashen as he then knew I had read all of the disgusting messages between them. "Who is Adriane?"

Trembling in the doorway, I waited for the outlandish story he was ready to concoct, twisting it to make it somehow become his truth, but I was surprised by his sudden inability to speak. I wasn't used to this. He always had an answer to everything, but today, I had caught him off guard. Why would he have given me his phone in the first place?

Did he want me to find those texts or was it as simple as he just forgot that he still had them on his phone when he handed it to me? It was almost as if I was supposed to find it. Not that he wanted me to find it but that I was supposed to see it. To wake me up. To let me know I deserved better. I was lost in thought as his nervous reactions only made him look more guilty.

"She's just a friend that I was going to train as she was interested in the business."

"Don't play me for a fool, Joe. I'm not that stupid. Those text messages were based on a lot more than friendship and you went on with how beautiful she was. If you want to be single, then why don't you?"

"Renee, I met her at one of the meetings the first week, and all of us as a group went to the casino for dinner. It wasn't just her and I. We talked about the business, but I was only being nice to her. She's nothing compared to you."

"You are such a liar, Joe!" I was angry and hurt and his response was so ridiculous, that it had escalated my anger even further. That day, I finally didn't care what he said. "That's the best you have, Joe? Quit lying to me! Tell me the truth!" I waited for a reply. Que the silence. He was trying to think of something to say, but he knew he had been caught and for the first time, he had no reply that could cover his seediness.

How old is she, Joe, and why did she have to ask her father if you could come out to see her? Does she live at home with her parents?" Just asking that made me feel sick. "No, she's twenty-three and lives with her boyfriend." Doing the math, I was disgusted at the thought that I was nineteen years older than her. How could I compete with that? I couldn't think straight anymore, but the Renee I once was, was gone. That Renee didn't exist anymore. I was so dependent on this man because of his manipulation, that his betrayal somehow made me feel as if I wasn't good enough.

"I didn't do anything with her, Renee. I would never cheat on you. I'm sorry I hurt you."

There it was. An apology. "Do you love me, Joe?"

"Of course I do. We wouldn't be living together if I didn't. I don't want anyone else. I love you so much. You have done more for me than any other woman ever has. I know I'm lucky to have you. I would never do anything to mess that up."

He was so good at lying to get his own way and to get himself out of trouble. I wanted so badly to believe him, but my gut told me otherwise. He was trying to reel me back in once again. His toxic but charming behavior and bouts of undying love blinded me to what was right in front of my face. Why did I need him? Thoughts of him being with another woman that was half my age made me nauseous. I couldn't wrap my mind around it.

With what dignity and strength I had left, I replied, "I know you never want to get married again but I do one day, and I'm not going to waste my life with someone who doesn't feel the same way. I want a life partner, someone I can grow old with, that won't cheat on me, someone I can depend on, someone who truly loves me, someone who is my best friend—someone I can call my husband. I've been with you for four years, and if you want to be single, then go ahead, be single, go party, or do whatever it is you do at all hours of the night after work. I deserve better."

I wanted him to just go away, to give me some space. I needed to think. Feeling the effects of his betrayal left me trying to think of where I would go. Where would I go with the kids? I would have to pull them out of their schools, and then what? Would I find a job? Could I provide for us all? Would we be okay? If it had just been me alone, I wouldn't have cared so much as I probably would have just left and stayed with a friend while I tried to sort my mess of a life out, but I had kids to think about. I wanted what was best for them. They were in top-rated schools, had nice friends, and we lived in an upscale neighborhood.

Life was good from the outside but a mess behind closed doors. Keeping them in this environment wasn't good either. What do I do? What about Joe's daughter, Callie, who he may get custody of? The courts were counting on me to help raise her as they knew we lived together and she would have a mother figure in her life, but what if I left? My heart was heavy with the emotional weight of what was and what was to be.

He asked, "How can I show you that you mean everything to me?"

"You can start by having no contact with her, deleting her name from your address book, and all of your text messages to one another." He picked up his phone as I watched his fingers hit the screen. "Done, it's deleted." I wanted proof as nothing he said would convince me he followed through with my demand. "Show me your phone. I want to see for myself."

He handed it to me without a word spoken. I quickly went through his contacts. Her name and number had disappeared. I then went to his text messages and all texts were gone as if they had never existed. I could only imagine he had felt defeated in that moment. Over the next few days, Joe did everything he could think of to apologize to me. I ignored him for some time as I couldn't even bring myself to look him in the face. He disgusted me, and yet, I still felt a longing for this man. Once again, I became overwhelmed by his outpouring of love and affection. He even bought me a car. It was a 2008 Mercedes sedan, which was known for its performance and comfort.

I had never asked for a new car, but we ended up at a pre-owned luxury dealership one day, which I was under the assumption we were there to just look at SUVs for our family. But Joe insisted that this was a better vehicle, and I couldn't find a way to tell him it wasn't as practical. I remember his words, "I want you to have the best. You deserve it. I love you so much. It's your car now so drive it home." He loved me. He really loved me.

Chapter Twelve

Who's Afraid of the Big Bad Wolf?

This year was the first year I didn't have the kids with me on Halloween and Hannah was with Christy, so Joe and I accepted an invite to a Halloween party. I went dressed in a sexy little red riding hood costume, and Joe went as the big bad wolf. We arrived at the party to meet up with his friend, Jeff and his girlfriend.

Not once had he told me that I looked great. I felt beautiful admiring my short red satin outfit that accentuated my curves, a tight bodice that showed some deep cleavage, followed by fishnet stockings with some sexy heels that completed the outfit. I definitely received some compliments, but not by him. He was in a fur-covered wolf's costume with a full wolf face mask and faux fur gloves. It was a perfect couple's costume. People loved it as we posed for some silly photos together. "I'm going to get us drinks," he said. I waited for him to return but later found him talking to a pretty blonde with a skimpy nurse's outfit on. Her costume didn't leave much to the imagination. Her breasts were almost bursting at the seams, and if she had bent over, there would be nothing left to shield her panties from showing. They were laughing and I don't know why, but that sickening feeling in my stomach returned once again. It was just a few weeks prior that I had found out about Joe's interest in Adriane and now here he was again, but this time flirting right in front of me.

I became angry at that moment, more out of hurt than real anger, but I couldn't believe he would be so disrespectful and show such cruel disregard for my feelings. Sociopaths lack self-conscience and don't experience remorse. He was freed up to do anything he wanted, which included anything bad that came to mind, regardless of the outcome.

I decided to walk over to both of them. "I've been waiting for you to return with a drink. What's the hold-up? Oh, let me guess," as I turned to walk away. I wanted him to know that he was being disrespectful and rude. I went to find Jeff's girlfriend. She was the only one I knew there. "Want to dance?", she asked, as she pulled me out on the dance floor. The song, *Dead Man's Party* started to play.

It brought me back to my high school days, and for the first time that night, I was having fun. A few drinks later, I became numb to the pain I had felt and was finally enjoying myself. After a few songs, we came back to the bar area, and there was Joe, standing there staring at me with his arms folded across his chest. What had I done? He was the one that just left me there and flirted shamelessly with another woman right in front of me. Why even go to a party together? Why didn't he tell me I looked sexy? There were so many— *Whys.*

The look on his face was enough to say that there would be hell to pay later. As we left the party, his vulgarities exploded once the car doors shut. He yelled at me the whole ride home. "Why are you so jealous? You had better accept the fact that I can talk to whoever I want to, whenever I want. There's always going to be someone prettier than you and someone better looking than me. That's just how it is!"

What the hell was he saying? I decided to see how the shoe fit on the other foot, and said, "Okay, then, I guess that means I could have stayed and talked to all the guys that told me how sexy I looked tonight, especially the one that told me I was so damn beautiful. I guess I have your permission then." I should have known that would have only made him angrier in the moment, but it felt so good to say. Whether he was trying to hurt me or degrade me, he blurted out, "I went to a strip club in Texas for one of the engineer's birthdays. Are you going to be jealous and insecure about that too?"

The sickening feeling returned as I sat there, shocked by what he had just said. "You're disgusting. If I were to do the same to you, you wouldn't have it. You just like to think you're so much better than everybody else and play by your own set of rules." He pulled into the driveway and turned towards me, his face inches from mine, but I held my ground, as I stared intensely at him. I felt I was looking right through him, almost like there was nothing there, his dark brown eyes were like a black hole, a void of all expression.

"Don't you forget it, honey!" I could feel his hot breath on my chin. My own anger had not subsided. The combination of his secret texts just a few weeks ago and now leaving me alone at the party to flirt with another woman was difficult to take. I was still hurting and now in a defensive mode. My brain told me to not back down. It was a normal reaction after keeping so much hurt and anger bottled up inside.

I decided to stay quiet, however; I believe that rage was the only way he could express himself. It was strange, but he was probably the most truthful when he was in a fit of absolute anger. I tuned him out and went somewhere else in my mind until I saw his face start to relax. He stepped out of the car, only to slam the door so hard, that the driver's side mirror completely shattered. This only enraged him more.

Somehow, it became my fault that he broke the mirror.

"See what you made me do!"

I couldn't deal with it anymore as I got out of the car.

"No one made you do anything. You did that yourself."

He went into the house screaming. "Joe, you need to calm down."

Looking at him, he still had on his wolf costume and he pathetically fit the part. His face tensed, and his eyes became enlarged with a predatory-type gaze. His body language told me that I should be ready for another round of emotional outbursts.

"Don't tell me to calm down!" You're just a jealous woman and I'm sick of it! I need a woman who can handle me talking to other women."

"Oh, is that what you call it? Talking?"

I knew I shouldn't have said it as soon as the words escaped my mouth, but I didn't want him to get away with saying such things to me. A part of me was scared of his reaction, and the other part just wanted to tell him how wrong he was. His goal was only to hurt me, and that's what he did next. I had a BlackBerry mobile phone at the time. Clutching it in my hand, it was my only lifeline if I needed to call someone.

He saw an opportunity and grabbed it from my hand, screaming, "You want to see what I call talking?", as he shoved the phone into the garbage disposal and flipped the switch on. I could hear the phone shattering into tiny pieces. Overwhelmed as extreme fear started to creep in, my chest tightened with a feeling of dread. I was in shock from his hateful behavior that traumatized my senses. How could he do this? Why did I allow his words to affect and control me? I ran crying to the bedroom and locked the bathroom door. I was confused. What do I do now? The house had gone quiet. Had he left? I didn't even care. I was sitting on the bathroom floor, and I heard him come into the room.

"Renee, open the door!"

"No, go away! Just leave me alone, Joe!" All I could think of was please just go away.

"If you don't open that door, I'll kick it down!" I was at such a low point that I didn't care what he did.

Thinking he would just walk away and calm down, he was true to his word and started to bang on the door.

"Open the door!"

"No, leave me alone!"

I could barely see through the tears that continued to flow. I was suddenly thrown against the wall with a forceful sweep of the door. He had kicked it in! My right hand had hit the wall so hard that it bent my wrist backward and the immediate agony I felt afterward made me scream out in pain. I was scared, alone, and without my phone to call anyone.

Attempting to defend myself from another blow, I looked down at my high heels and removed one, throwing it at him to get him to stop, hoping I could shake him out of his psychotic rage. It's all I could do or think of at the moment. The tip of the heel hit him in the chest and instead of reacting with more violence, his demeanor changed in the split of a second as his body relaxed. "Are you okay?"

His reaction caught me off guard as he suddenly went calm at the sound of me sobbing. "I'll go get some ice for it. It's going to get swollen." The pain from turning my wrist was unbearable. I couldn't move it at all. Joe came back minutes later with some ice and a wrist brace. Where had that come from? I didn't dare ask, fearing more of his violent outbursts. I just sat there whimpering, as I watched my wrist slowly start to become inflamed through the painful tenderness.

After an hour of Joe assuring me that my wrist would heal, he gently placed the brace on it. I cried even more, now realizing he had destroyed my phone. I was terrified. It was the only thing I could count on in an emergency and now it was gone. He suddenly went from being extremely angry and negative to telling me all the things he knew that would make me stay.

"I would never hurt you, Renee. We will get you a new phone tomorrow and a much better one then you had." That was his way of apologizing. He would do that often to woo me back after an argument, switching back and forth between extreme charm and extreme threats to get what he wanted. He knew my weak spots and vulnerabilities.

I couldn't even look at him, as he continued to pour out his overly dramatic pleas of love and how we were meant to be together. "I love you. I need you. I would die if you left me." He had no clue what love meant. Why did I stay? He had betrayed me, and I knew he was bad for me, yet I still loved him and didn't know how to live without him.

Chapter Thirteen

Bringing Callie Home

The days that followed were difficult and I tried keeping my distance from Joe. I wanted to believe that he felt remorse for what he had done, but sociopaths don't feel remorse or empathy for their actions. However, he was good at faking it. He knew he had done some irrevocable damage. He became overly attentive and fixated on my every need. He even took my car to a repair shop and had the side mirror fixed, making sure that I was happy with his achievement.

"Do you like your mirror?" I could only bring myself to say, "Yes, and thank you for fixing it." I really didn't feel I should have thanked him as he was the one who broke it in a fit of rage, but I wasn't about to go there. His outpouring of gifts and staying home for dinner lasted for a short while, but he knew I couldn't move my wrist very well. Our friends and family just thought he was this great guy taking care of the woman he loved. No one knew.

The date for the final court hearing was approaching, and Joe asked that I attend it with him in Texas. If he was granted sole custody of Callie, he thought it would be better if I was by his side. I agreed as my heart went out to a little girl who had lost her mother and now possibly her grandparents as well. They were the only family she had known since she was born, besides Joe's temporary visits from time to time.

We were not only waiting to hear what the court would decide on Callie's future but what ours would be as well. It would forever be changed if we brought Callie home, but we both knew that she would have a better quality of life than the one she was living. There were many things we had to face together, including how Hannah was going to react to having a sister and no longer being Joe's only child. She was already starving for Joe's attention, and I could only imagine it would be even more so if he was granted custody with everyone welcoming Callie to the family.

Time seemed to tick by slowly leading up to that emotional day. We entered the courtroom together hand in hand and felt confident we would be leaving that day with Callie. I looked around to see Desiree's parents sitting to the left of the room, but there was no sign of Desiree. It sickened me to think she wasn't there to fight for her child. Where was she?

It made me want to bring Callie home even more. This poor little girl never even really knew her mother. I thought as she grew up, who would she have to talk to about all the things girls go through from the changes in their bodies to boy troubles? She sure couldn't talk to Joe about it. He would have dismissed it. I wanted to be there for her as a mother.

The judge walked in and came quickly to his decision, based on what was in the best interest for Callie. Joe was being given sole, legal, and physical custody of Callie, provided that he took her to a child therapist who could help her through this emotional transition. The sobbing of her grandparents was heartbreaking. Desiree never appeared, which looked even worse to the court, as it was stated she was not allowed to have any physical or verbal contact with Callie at all.

We were happy but we knew there would be months of therapy and many changes in the household. We were to go and pick up Callie at three-o-clock that day. The grandparents had until then to say their goodbyes. It was hard to be so happy when you had another family that had to let Callie go, and may not ever see her again. Joe looked like he had just won the lottery, smiling victoriously. Walking out of the courthouse, he whispered, "I'll never have to pay that woman child support ever again." He believed any child support he had sent Desiree in the past was being used for drugs and didn't go towards Callie's care.

He surprisingly turned towards me and held me tight. "Thanks for coming here with me today. Your support means a lot and I love you so much." It felt good to hear him say that. "Of course, Joe. I want the best for Callie, and I'm here for you." Rob, Callie's grandfather, approached us. He had written down Callie's daily routine and the medications she took for her allergies, wiping away his tears as he spoke.

It was heart-wrenching to witness. He looked at me with a half-smile. "Please love her as much as we do." I couldn't help but reach out to hug him and whisper, "I will. Don't worry. She'll be very loved." I wanted to cry for them, for Callie, for our children at home, for everyone. It was a very emotional day. Picking Callie up, while the family said their goodbyes went smoothly. She was a brave little girl, not even crying as we drove away; however, she didn't really understand what was going on.

Joe thought she would like to get ice cream, so I sat in an ice cream parlor eating a fudge cone with her while he was outside on his phone. I was used to his more than frequent phone calls by now. She had hardly spoken a word since we picked her up. "Do you like bubble gum ice cream?", she asked, smiling with a shade of pink around her lips. "I love bubble gum ice cream," I said, giggling from the expression she was making as she stuck out her ice cream cone for me to taste. It was such a sweet moment. Her innocence melted my heart.

I quickly licked the side. "Mmm, that is so good. Thank you for sharing." She smiled shyly. The nurturing part of me as a mother quickly took over. Joe abruptly walked back in and confirmed he had booked Callie a seat on our return flight home. We were all set. No one was at the house when we arrived home as Ryan and Emma had gone with their father and Hannah was with her mother. We were planning to introduce Callie to them the next day. We got Callie ready for bed and tucked her in. It was a lot for her to absorb. She was scared and didn't know where she was. We were strangers to her. I laid down next to Joe in bed and heard Callie start to cry.

Before I could even respond, Joe shouted, "You should go console her. She needs a woman to tell her it's going to be okay, not me!" Sigh. I could feel it. This was how it was all going to be. Nothing was going to change with him. It made me want to protect Callie even more, and that night, I laid with her in her bed, telling her about all the fun things we could do together as a family. Everything would be okay.

The next day, Callie met Hannah, Emma, and Ryan. She loved the girls, but I could tell she wasn't too sure of Ryan. We knew that she had been exposed to some dire situations when she was with her mother on the streets in Texas, and I quickly got the impression that she was scared of men. We had been told she might have witnessed some possible drug dealings and who knows what else in the places she was found in at times with Desiree. It seemed to me that men scared her, even Joe.

Over time, she warmed up to Ryan and finally felt a sense of comfort. It was hard for her when she first started pre-school and went to see the therapist. She didn't want to let go of my hand, and she was always by my side. On many occasions, when she had to go in with the therapist, she would run back to me and plop on my lap. The therapist was a wonderful lady that could tell Callie had been through a traumatic experience. She was patient and knew how to talk to her.

Joe started to travel more frequently, scouting out other locations for his tour business, so I was the one who ended up taking Callie to most of her appointments. Soon, she was calling me mama, and I became that mother lion, just wanting to protect her cub. I loved her as my own. People would frequently tell us that she looked so much like me, which was funny, given the situation. I would just smile and say, "Thank you."

Callie would soon, however, find her courage to test the waters, as she could throw some wild temper tantrums if she didn't get her way, but she could also put Joe in his place at times when he started pitching one of his many fits. Under the circumstances and knowing it would get back to Callie's therapist, Joe retreated from his wild outbursts over that time and acted on his best behavior. It was a refreshing change.

Chapter Fourteen

The Bar Proposal

Life was a whirlwind and exhausting for the next few months as we adjusted to our schedules with school and therapy sessions. I was dropping off and picking up the kids at three different schools, between the pre-school, middle and high school, answering business calls on my mobile, taking Callie to her therapy appointments, and trying my best to keep some distance from Joe. I stopped asking him where he had been on the nights that he came home late or what time he would be home.

We could both sense that there was a shift in our relationship, and as if trying to reel me back in once again, he asked me to go to Mexico with him and another couple that was friends of his. Everyone we associated with were now his friends, but he just looked at it as his friends were now mine.

"Where would we stay?"

"My friend, Stan, and his wife own a timeshare at an all-inclusive resort in Cabo San Lucas. It's a presidential suite. I already paid for it and told them we would go. It's just you and me. No kids on this trip."

This felt odd. Why did he suddenly want to go to Mexico with me? I really felt that I had no choice in the matter since he already confirmed with them and paid for the trip, but at the same time, I thought it would do us both good. Maybe he was really trying to make up for all the things that had happened in the last few months.

"Who's going to watch the kids?"

"We'll figure it out, Renee."

That's how Joe was. He just expected everyone to jump over hoops for him to do what he wanted, booking the trip before we even had childcare figured out. Thankfully, we were able to coordinate childcare for the kids quickly. Why didn't I feel excited about going? I wasn't even sure what to feel. All I had felt lately was emotionally numb and distant as if I had all but given up on being happy and truly loved, and Joe must have sensed it.

We arrived in Cabo San Lucas in February. It felt good breaking the routine of things and arriving at a sunny destination. The weather was seventy-five degrees and perfect to just lay out on the beach. Joe was very attentive and loving. He had turned on his charm, and I loved feeling like I was his queen. I didn't want that day to end.

We had a certain spot on the beach that we would come to every day and noticed the same group of older women there. They were funny, and you couldn't help but laugh at their stories. We all became beach buddies after one too many drinks. I started to feel good again, almost if I had woken up from a deep sleep. Joe had made a reservation for us to go swimming with dolphins at the marina. I was over the moon as I had loved dolphins since I was a little girl and never thought I may be swimming with them.

The highlight of this dolphin encounter was a dorsal fin tow across the water and interacting one on one with them. The water was extremely cold, but it was an exhilarating experience. After a fun photo session with the dolphins, we set out to leave. I was under the impression we were going back to the hotel when Joe suddenly said, "Let's go to the diamond store in town." The look on my face must have been one of shock as I almost tripped and fell over my own feet.

"What? Why do you want to look at diamonds?" My heart was pounding anxiously as I waited for his reply.

"To look at rings," he said, smirking as if waiting to tell me his secret.

I still wasn't sure what he meant. Was he looking for a ring for me or for him? Was he implying he wanted to get married? No, that couldn't be. This was a man who said he never wanted to get married and made sure that I knew that from the beginning. Of course, I knew that this was a man that could say one thing and do another, so anything was possible.

"Wait, you want to get a diamond ring?"

"Yes, for you, and only the best ring if we're going to get married."

"What? Married? I thought you didn't want to get married?" My heart felt like it was beating through my chest. I was sure he could hear it.

"I want to marry you, Renee. You are the one woman who understands me, and I want us to be together forever, but I'm going to ask you the right way later tonight. Right now, I just want you to pick out whatever ring you want."

I couldn't comprehend what was happening. Why did he want to get married now? Why did he change his mind on marriage? Was he going to ask me to marry him out of guilt for what he had done? Was he scared of losing me and did he really see me as someone he wanted to grow old with? I was shocked and confused and should have been ecstatic about his planning to propose to me, but instead, I felt perplexed by it all.

I tried shaking off the feeling as we walked hand in hand to an upscale jewelry store. It was one of the most beautiful and elegant jewelry stores I had ever seen. I tried on many diamond rings and finally chose a beautiful princess cut ring with a diamond baguette band. My hand was shaking as I made my selection. Joe handed the sales representative his credit card, smiling nervously as I removed it for them to size my finger. "Thank you, Joe. It's a beautiful ring."

He laughed. "Well, I haven't asked you yet."

The thought must have sent a mischievous little smile to his lips as he grabbed me with one arm to pull me into him. The awkwardness I had been feeling vanished as he held me tightly. Once back at the hotel, I noticed that he didn't mention proposing that evening to his friends but did say that he wanted to have dinner alone with me. I honestly thought he would propose later that evening on the beach. It would just be the two of us.

After showering from the dolphin experience, we returned to the marina, which was alive with nightlife from vacationers due to the variety of popular seafood restaurants, lively bars, and high-end boutique shops. Of course, all I could think of was the ring Joe had in his coat pocket. Was he going to ask me soon? We walked along the boardwalk, looking at the wide array of fishing boats while enjoying the spectacular sunset over the water.

We decided to dine at a place called the Tiki Bar. It was a quaint little spot that was famous for its sushi and fish tacos. Just a few feet away was a local musician who was playing his guitar and singing pop songs in English. We were singing along and noticed a large crowd of people at another table. They were a lively bunch, singing loudly and having fun.

Once the musician went on break, Joe stood up, and I thought we were leaving, so I stood to leave. He looked at me, and said, "We're not leaving quite yet." I saw him reach in his coat pocket, and my heart jumped into my throat. Was he going to ask me in front of all of these people? He approached the musician and whispered something, then the musician handed him his microphone. All I could think of was, *"Oh shit, he's going to ask me over the microphone."* I was light-headed and somehow felt like I was waiting to be completely embarrassed.

"Excuse me, everyone." The mic echoed loudly, and the room went silent. "I wanted to get everyone's attention here because I want to shout it to the rooftop on how much I love this woman sitting right here. Renee, you are my world, and from the beginning, I knew we were soulmates." My throat went dry and I couldn't swallow. I could see the tears starting to form in his eyes. "You are a beautiful person and a wonderful mother, and I know that things haven't been easy. You've stood by me and supported me through it all, and I know that I want to grow old with you, no matter what life brings us."

Standing there with tears streaming down his face, he looked so genuine and his words sounded so heartfelt. I could hear some oohs and aws from some of the women in the room as he continued with his grand gestures of love. "My grandfather had told me to marry someone one day that I love as much as he loved my grandmother, and I know that person is you." Now incessantly crying and looking emotionally love-struck, he dropped to one knee, took out the ring, and said, "Renee, I will love you forever. Will you be my wife?" The room fell silent as if everyone had disappeared, and Joe was left waiting for my response.

"Yes, Joe, of course, I'll marry you!" He hugged me and I could feel his body tremble, as I told him I would love him forever. I looked at my hand as he placed the ring on my finger. It was beautiful. We were engaged! The sound of the room's applause and whistles could be heard down the boardwalk. The musician congratulated us with a love song, and the large crowd of people we had been singing along with celebrated our future happiness with rounds of drinks and congratulatory toasts. A few women even came over to say how sweet Joe's proposal was and how it teared them up. I was happy, but I didn't have the emotional reaction that I thought I was going to have. I knew he had planned to ask me at some point that evening, but I was very calm and still questioned why he had asked me now.

Maybe I was overthinking all of this. I suddenly thought of the children and telling them that we would be getting married. How would Ryan feel about being a big brother to Hannah and Callie? How would Emma and Hannah like being sisters? They got along so well but I wasn't sure. Or maybe, Joe did this so I could have legal guardianship of Callie if anything ever happened to him. The questions kept circulating in my head.

Chapter Fifteen

Let the Games Begin

We had two days left in our little paradise by the ocean. Our friends, Stan and Lisa, that we had traveled with were somewhat upset that we had not invited them to dinner the night before to celebrate our engagement. I wasn't sure what Joe's' reasoning was for it either, but Joe had known Stan for years, so maybe he had told him in the past that he would never get married again and now, here he was proposing. I couldn't help but think that maybe he felt embarrassed by proposing to me in front of his friends but was comfortable enough proposing in front of complete strangers.

It was another beautiful day to lay out on the beach. Stan and Lisa decided to join us. We found our normal spot and noticed that a few of the ladies we had chatted with previously were there as well. One of them was an older woman, who looked to be in her late sixties. Her name was Evelyn. She shared with us that she owned a carnival ride company and traveled frequently to where the next carnival destination would take her. She did well for herself, and I found her to be quite fascinating with all of the interesting stories she shared with us about her life.

At this time, I was still trying to answer business calls but the hotel had spotty WIFI, so I occasionally had to walk to a designated area to listen to voicemails and return phone calls. I left Joe sitting there and let him know that I would be back after returning any missed calls. When I returned, he was gone. I asked Lisa, "Where did Joe go?"

"Oh, he went with Stan to the beach bar to get some drinks." I thought nothing of it, so I enjoyed listening to the camaraderie between the group of ladies. I found it difficult to talk; I was laughing so hard with their hilarious one-liners and stories. It had been an hour since I returned, and there was still no sign of Joe. Lisa wondered where Stan was as well but brushed it off as the two had probably wandered around the hotel talking or maybe they sat at the bar to enjoy a drink. Again, I thought nothing of it as I looked at the beautiful ring on my finger.

Since Joe wasn't back yet, I told Lisa that I would go to the beach bar for drinks. As I walked into the little bar, I saw a woman sitting in a booth. She had long black hair, brown eyes, and a glowing tan. She was attractive, but it wasn't her that had caught my attention. The person with his back to me sitting in the booth with her was Joe. There was no sign of Stan. "Hi, Joe. Did you lose your way to the bar to get us drinks? You've been gone a long time."

Joe's face flushed as he tried to make up some excuse on why he was sitting with that woman. "I was hungry and decided to eat lunch. This is Megan. She is from California, and she's traveling alone and has no one to hang out with. I was just keeping her company. Do you want to join us?" What the hell had just happened? I couldn't even make sense of what he had just said and why he decided to brush me off to sit there with her for what must have been almost two hours since I had gone to retrieve voicemails. My blood started to boil.

The only reason he was sitting there was that she was attractive and alone, and he wanted to flirt with her, and who knows what else. "No, I'm not joining you. I came to get drinks for Lisa and me since you never came back with them or with Stan. By the way, where is Stan?" Joe was short with his reply. "He went back to the room to lie down for a bit." Looking at Megan, who looked to be in her mid-twenties, I couldn't help but feel that Joe wanted more than friendship with her. It was the same ole Joe.

"Well, nice to meet you, Megan. Enjoy your friendly chat, and oh, by the way, did Joe share the wonderful news with you that we just got engaged last night?" I couldn't help it. It just poured out of my mouth. I was hurt by his actions and wanted him to feel at least a little humiliation. "Enjoy your lunch." I quickly stormed out, leaving Joe and his newfound friend. Trying to make sense of what had just happened, I found a pool bar and came back with drinks for Lisa and me.

"Did you find them?"

"I did. Stan went back to the room to lie down, and Joe apparently made a new friend. A pretty one. They're having lunch together."

She bolted straight up, removing her sunglasses. "What? Why the hell would he be in the bar with someone else?"

Tears started to form as I thought of the many lies that he had fabricated over the years. This felt no different. "I'm not sure. I guess you will have to ask him." What I didn't realize is that the group of ladies next to us had heard our conversation and one of them commented, "That is crazy." I was about to reply when I saw Joe approaching us. He didn't look happy. "How could you embarrass me like that?" Weren't you supposed to be answering calls?"

Here it came. His anger was on display for everyone to see. I wasn't going to be bullied in front of my new friends, but the anxiety and disappointment from his actions proved to be too much. The tears started flowing, and with a quivering voice, I replied, "If you had been here instead of flirting with that woman in the beach bar, you would have known that I returned phone calls and booked some reservations. You were gone for almost two hours! Lisa even thought you were with Stan, and to my surprise, you were sitting with some woman."

Everyone was silent, as Lisa threw Joe a disapproving look. His jaw tightened as he waved his fists. "How dare you talk to me like that! I was just being nice to someone that was here by themselves. You need to get your shit together and stop being so jealous. You're acting like a crazy woman!"

I had to defend myself. I just had to. "I am? So, let me ask you something then. You and Megan were talking for quite some time. You even know where she was from. Did you tell her you had just got engaged last night?" I waited for his response.

He turned around to see our new friends staring him down and suddenly realized he was surrounded by women that had heard his ridiculous excuse. The look he gave me was pure evil as he walked away in anger. What was I in for later? Was he going to call off the engagement now after pulling his little stunt? It must have gotten to him as thirty minutes later, he was back, sat down on the lounge chair next to me, and spoke to Lisa about the cruise ship that had docked nearby.

What the hell? I thought maybe he would apologize for his crude behavior, but an apology never came. Instead, I received a new opal necklace he had purchased from a jewelry vendor on the beach. That was his way of apologizing, and I also believe it was just another performance for anyone that had witnessed his angry outbursts. I had many gifts from Joe over the years, gifts that said, *I'm sorry*. My jewelry box was full of his apologies.

As we spoke of the buffet dinner that evening, our friends decided we should all get a table together. Lisa and

I thought it was a great idea, but there was no comment from Joe. That evening Joe and I met up with Stan and Lisa and found our friends at a table. The buffet was a spectacular spread of the freshest seafood with plenty of Mediterranean and Mexican dishes that would make your mouth water. While Joe was talking to Stan, I excused myself to go to the buffet line. When I returned, Joe's expression had radically changed as if someone had just smacked him across his face.

As he left to get his food, Lisa leaned over to me and whispered, "Joe just got chewed out."

"What are you talking about?"

"Evelyn gave him a piece of her mind on the way he treated you today and how disgraceful it was. If that wasn't enough, she lectured him on how he should never treat someone he loves like that."

Evelyn, the older woman who had shared her life story with me earlier, had stood up for me. Someone had finally stood up for me, and it felt so good. Here was a woman who had gone through many things in her life and she wasn't afraid to stand up to Joe. I was grateful for her being there. Joe needed to hear that from someone, and now, someone besides myself had voiced their concern over his outbursts. I looked over at her and she just smiled. *Thank you, Evelyn*, I said in my head, hoping somehow that she knew what I was thinking as Joe sat back down. My spirit had been lifted by her act of heroism. At that time, she was my hero.

Joe must have been caught off guard and felt humiliated by her words as he suddenly mentioned that he didn't feel well and was going back to the room to lie down. I knew it wasn't that. He just couldn't bear the fact that he was proven wrong by his actions and someone had told him that to his face. I stood to go back to the room with him, but he stopped me. "No, Renee, you stay with Stan and Lisa and enjoy the band after dinner. I just don't feel well and just want to lie down." I'm not sure if he wanted me to insist that I go up to the room with him, so he didn't feel guilty in front of others if I left with him, but I didn't. "Okay, I hope you feel better."

As he walked away, I wondered if he was really going to the room, but I was enjoying the moment of satisfaction too much to be concerned with it. Stan, Lisa, and I enjoyed the rest of the evening with our new friends, dancing on the beach into the wee hours of the night.

Joe said nothing to me the next day about what Evelyn might have said to him, but thanks to Lisa, I knew. It was time to go home. I kept thinking about the kids and how they would react to our news. As we boarded the plane, I didn't want to think about what had happened the day before, but I knew the head games would continue. I closed my eyes, wanting to shut out the world, attempting to drown out the negative emotions that continued to resurface. What could I say at that moment confined in close quarters? I felt him take my hand and hold it tightly. Was that supposed to make me feel better? It didn't.

Chapter Sixteen

Marrying the Man Behind the Mask

After our return home, the daily routine of things quickly fell back into place. Nothing had changed except we still had to tell the kids of our engagement. We were already a family, but to me, it now felt even more like a connection. We were going to be bonded by marriage. Joe and I decided to sit everyone down that evening and tell them before we told other family members. Their innocent little faces expressed concern as we told them that we had something to tell them.

Joe looked at me as if I needed to be the one to tell them in my own way. Taking a deep breath, I said, "Something happened while we were in Mexico." Hannah amusingly shouted, "I know what it is! You're pregnant!"

"Oh goodness, no!", as we all laughed, "But you all are going to be brothers and sisters."

I waited. Ryan's eyes widened while Hannah and Emma looked confused. Callie wasn't sure what any of it quite meant as she sat there quietly listening. Ryan looked at the girls in disbelief. "Geez, you guys! It means they're getting married!" Joe and I both weren't expecting the reaction that followed. Emma and Hannah started giggling and hugging each other. "We're going to be sisters!" They both started crying, laughing through their tears, and watching them, it brought tears to my eyes as well. It was so very heartfelt that even Joe had tears in his, basking happily in that moment. Their sweet reactions to our engagement made everything feel right with the world.

"So, when are you getting married?", asked Emma. "Well, we're not sure yet," I replied. As if Joe sensed my hesitation, he blurted out, "Why don't we get married back in Cabo San Lucas in May? That's a slow time for the tour business, so we can take the kids and let them have fun on the beach." That was all the kids needed to hear. "We're going to Mexico!", shouted Hannah. I pondered over a wedding on the beach and thought how nice it would be if the kids were a part of it. I loved that idea.

"Maybe we can get married on a private beach there?"

"Anything you want, Renee. Just let me know how much it's all going to cost." Of course, it was back to how much it was going to cost him. I started to research beach weddings and compared a house rental to a hotel since we would need multiple rooms. I researched airfare and the cost of transfers, and I finally found the perfect place. There was a beautiful three-bedroom villa in a gated community. It was steps away to a private beach where we could get married at sunset. The cost was less than booking multiple rooms at a hotel on the popular, Medano Beach.

After discussing the choices with Joe, he agreed to the rental, but only on one condition. He wanted me to sign a pre-nuptial agreement. I couldn't help but feel insulted, but Joe convinced me that he only wanted it to protect his business since Christy had tried to take part of his business from him throughout their divorce. "I just don't want to go through that again. I have a lot on the line, and I need to have a way to protect myself. Anything can happen, even though I don't believe you would ever do something like that to me."

I felt like a bombshell had been dropped on me. I understood his concern for protecting his business as he had built it from nothing and he had thousands of dollars in equipment at stake, but it also meant I would receive nothing if we were divorced. This concerned me since I ran the business. He had told others that I was his operations manager. He had never paid me a salary, and I felt signing a pre-nuptial with these stipulations would be highly unfair.

"I'll sign it, Joe, but since I run your business and would be walking away with nothing to show for putting my blood, sweat, and tears into it, I would ask that you pay me a lump sum that we can agree to, only so that I could get on my feet if I were to be on my own. I would have to find another job and a new place to live, and by the way, I would never try to take your business away from you, but I need to protect myself as well."

I thought he would be upset with my response, but surprisingly he agreed, which in retrospect would not have impacted his business whatsoever since, over the past two years, the business had done very well financially. I had now been working for him for five years and felt this was more than fair going forward.

At least now I had something to fall back on if things ever went south in our marriage. We may have some difficult times ahead but never did I believe for one second that we would divorce. We were soulmates. I loved him, and he constantly told me that I was the only woman he had ever loved. He was very convincing, and I still believed him. Once the pre-nuptial was singed, Joe gave me the go-ahead to secure our trip for the last week of May. I ordered beautiful ocean blue matching dresses for the girls and a dark blue shirt with black slacks for Ryan. Due to our budget, I purchased a pre-owned satin wedding dress from a woman online.

It was a beautiful backless dress, with a V-neck neckline and spaghetti straps, and it fit my curves perfectly. I didn't even need to have it altered as if it were made just for me. I was happy that I had found the perfect dress for our wedding. At the time, my father had told me he was too scared to travel to Mexico, but his fears were valid. He had never been to Cabo San Lucas and I didn't want him to feel uncomfortable so I asked my son if he could walk me down the aisle. His beaming smile gave me my answer. "Of course, I will mom." He made me so proud to be his mother. My heart was full.

A month later, slowly but steadily, my reality started to change. Joe had grown distant and seemed distracted. He became irritable and defensive and became increasingly manipulative to the point that I started questioning if he really wanted to get married and if all this had been an act, but with what reasoning, I wasn't sure. The business had slowed down and the money wasn't coming in like before; however, it was typical for this time of year based on weather. I then thought maybe he had second thoughts on signing the pre-nuptial, but why didn't he just talk to me about it?

Joe had decided he wanted to go deep-sea fishing a day prior to everyone else arriving in Cabo, so he wanted to take Ryan on the fishing trip with him along with his best friend. "*A guy's trip.*" I booked the airfare and rental so they would arrive a day earlier, and the girls and I would plan to fly out the day after together. I was concerned he may have a little bachelor party of his own before I arrived, and I didn't want my teenage son exposed to any seedy activity. "No strip clubs, Joe, especially since Ryan is with you."

Joe laughed, looking at me as if I was crazy, but I honestly wasn't sure what he might be planning. "I would never take Ryan to a strip club, Renee. Give me some credit. We're just going deep sea fishing, that's it."

Joe had a way of being very convincing with his words and twisting the truth in a way that I no longer trusted my own judgment or reasoning at times. There were red flags all around me, but I always seemed to brush them off, ignoring my own sense of self as I was no longer the same person that had entered the relationship. I didn't know then that Joe's reason for really marrying me was that he wanted someone he could control, a person that would be so committed to him, who he could blame for everything, while he created a positive image of himself to the outside world.

No one knew of the destruction he was capable of. No one knew the man behind the mask. I was so dependent on him that I wasn't even aware of how dangerous he could truly be. Of course, I continued to believe that I was special to him and he really loved me. A man that I thought was my soulmate and would do anything for me. I still didn't know then what a sociopath was.

It was a week before our wedding, and we had gone through all of the paperwork for the wedding officiant to perform a civil ceremony on the beach. The kids had their passports, and we were all excited. Joe, on the other hand, was still acting defensively. He wanted to take out cash at the bank for expenses in Cabo and returned with a stack of cash in his hand. I was in the bedroom, trying to decide what clothes to bring, and he abruptly shouted, "Here's the cash!" He threw it over the bed and dollar bills went flying everywhere. "I hope you're happy!", and just like that, he stormed out of the room.

I was shocked by his outburst. Was this made to make me feel guilty for getting married? Why was he so mad? What should have been a joyous time in our lives turned into a deeply hurtful one, filled with dread. What had I done? I didn't want to marry someone that didn't really want to get married. He was bitter and angry, and I didn't know what I should do. "Why are you so angry at me? "Do you want me to cancel the trip, Joe?"

"No, it's too late now! I'm spending thousands of dollars at a time the business is slow but you wanted this beach wedding!" I was mortified. "What? That's not fair! How could you say that? The cost of this whole trip for all of us combined was three-thousand dollars. Your friend, Jeff, just had his third wedding in Vegas and said they spent seventeen thousand. I thought you were okay with it. Why are you attacking me now, before we leave?"

"What, Renee? I don't make enough money for you now? Maybe, you should have married Jeff!" The sound of his words echoed in my head. I felt sick to my stomach. I knew there was no winning this argument that he had started. I ran to the bathroom, which had recently become my quiet place, and closed the door. I could hear Joe mumbling about how I didn't understand and then denying that he ever suggested getting married in Cabo. He was now cursing loudly with every other word being fu** this and fu** that, telling me that I was delusional and making it seem like I was crazy for even asking him why he was acting this way.

I sat on the bathroom floor and cried. All I wanted was for this man to love me and for all of us to be a happy family. I wanted our children to feel loved and protected, but I knew deep down they had heard his outbursts and many of our arguments behind closed doors. There were times that I walked out of the bedroom after one of his crazy tangents and all the bedroom doors in the house would be closed. It saddened me that our children suffered through his anger too, not wanting to hear some of the hurtful and outlandish things he would say. They tried their best to tune him out.

Joe never apologized. He had left with Ryan for his fishing trip with what seemed to be a chip on his shoulder. Why was he making me feel like this the week we were getting married? I should have been happy, but I just couldn't get past what he had said. I went to bed that night and cried. I wondered if it was too late to back out, and what would happen with the sisterly love Hannah and Emma shared, not to mention how Callie would feel not having a mother around. I had to toughen up and find some strength. My happiness didn't matter anymore. The children needed me, and some part of me thought Joe needed me too.

Once I arrived in Cabo with the girls, we had a driver waiting in the airport for us with our name on a sign. A feeling of relief washed over me. I had only come here with

Joe and felt safe but traveling by myself with young girls gave me a bad case of anxiety. This was also the first time we would be staying somewhere I had never been. Ryan, Joe, and his best friend, Dave, were waiting at the rental house when we arrived. Looking at them, one could tell they had a fisherman's tan. Their faces were bright red with a large red line around their necks from where their t-shirts must have been.

"Did you guys have fun fishing? Catch any big fish?" Ryan replied excitedly, "It was so cool! We caught the biggest Mahi-Mahi ever and some Yellow Tail too! Oh, and he's having our tour guide filet and cook it for us tonight! Isn't that awesome, mom?" I loved seeing Ryan so happy and excited about his fishing adventure. "Wow! That is wonderful, Ryan. I can't wait to have it for dinner tonight." Joe glanced my way while Hannah and Callie ran over to hug him. Was I going to get the silent treatment? I couldn't tell. This all felt wrong somehow, but maybe I was just overreacting with what had been going through my mind the night before.

The villa was breathtaking, as we walked into what would be our home for the next week. It had a chef's kitchen and a spacious open floor plan, which was perfect for keeping our eyes on Callie. She mostly followed Hannah and Emma around, but they liked their own space. We were getting married in two days, and my mother and stepfather would be arriving the next day. After watching the kids splashing around in the backyard pool, I ventured upstairs to find lounge chairs on the rooftop. It was quiet there and a scenic place to relax and watch the sunset.

The sky turned into a glorious palette of colors. Taking in its golden glow, everything slowed down for a moment as I was overcome with a feeling of peace and calm. I wanted to bask in that moment for a while, but just as I started to lay back in my chair, I heard a commotion from behind. I swung around to see Joe standing there with a beer in his hand. "Here, I brought you a beer," he said, as he put his arms around me. This was his first attempt of showing any kind of affection since blaming me for booking the beach wedding.

I wasn't quite sure what to say to him, fearing that another argument would ensue. "Thanks." I'm sure he could feel my agitation and my unhappiness stemming from his recent behavior. "What's wrong, Renee?" How could he even ask me that? "Nothing. I'm fine." I tried shaking it all off, as I walked away and downstairs to sit with the kids. The tour guide had filleted our fish and was cooking it on the barbeque for a wonderful seafood dinner. The kids got a huge kick out of it, and it felt good seeing them so happy. I had waited for this week to come, and now that it was here, I found myself forcing a smile for everyone. No one ever questioned my more-than-forced smiles, not my parents or my children.

As I awoke on our wedding day, I was full of mixed emotions. This was it! I felt like a nervous wreck but spending time with the kids on the beach and getting a nice golden glow the day before had felt good. I finally felt rested. I looked forward to getting my hair and makeup done that day. I hadn't felt pretty in a long time, partially because my self-esteem was shot and partially because Joe could pick on any little flaw about my hair or makeup or how I dressed. I rarely heard him say that I was pretty. If I asked, I would normally receive a response, *"You look fine."*

Now, here I was, with our children and our parents in paradise, and I wanted this day to be a special one to remember, not tainted by anger, distrust, and fear. I put it all to the side. Joe and his friend, Dave, had to get dressed upstairs and left to go down to the beach to meet with the officiant. The girls had left with my mother to take their places as bridesmaids as my stepfather and Ryan walked down together. It was just me now. The hair and makeup artist had finished. I was eager to see what masterpiece he had created.

As I looked in the mirror, I gasped, pleasantly surprised by the person looking back at me. I felt glamorously exquisite. My hair was delicately swept up with mini ivory roses weaved in throughout the back. My hazel eyes were highlighted with hues of brown and gold eyeshadows and liner. I didn't recognize myself. I slipped on my dress and took it all in. I felt beautiful and somewhat panicked at the same time. Was this just pre-wedding jitters or something else?

My inner voice told me that Joe loved me and that he wouldn't have asked me to marry him otherwise. I convinced myself I was just once again overreacting and that things would be better soon. My normal, rational way I use to think or contemplate on things no longer existed. This was the only normal I knew, so even though I can see how toxic it was now, I didn't see it like that then. I wanted his love and I wanted my family. It was our wedding day. We would say our vows and live by them.

I walked the steps down to the beach. Joe's back was to me as I had not wanted him to see me until Ryan walked me down to him. The children were smiling at the sight of my arrival. Our parents looked on joyfully as a bridal song started to play. I wrapped my arm around Ryan's as he walked me towards Joe. Ryan looked so proud to fill that role. My heart felt as if it were going to burst. Joe turned around. I was startled by his reaction as he started to cry. As Ryan took his place, Joe and I faced each other. I took in that moment as the calming sounds of the ocean hitting the shoreline calmed my nervousness.

Holding my hands, Joe and I said our vows to each other as our family looked on. He continued to shake his head side to side, smiling through his tears, telling me how beautiful I was. The moment was upon us as we heard the wedding officiant say, "You may kiss the bride." With a quick peck on the lips, it was over. I had always imagined this long drawn-out passionate, Hollywood worthy kiss, but it was brief. I wondered at that moment if he was embarrassed to show any public display of affection. I had never known him to be that way before.

We then were shuttled to a restaurant that had the most spectacular views, not to mention the best seafood in the area. I felt different. I was Joe's wife. Joe sat across the table from me, talking to his father. It wasn't what I had envisioned as a little girl marrying her prince charming, but then again, I told myself, life wasn't a fairytale.

Chapter Seventeen

An Unexpected Move

That summer proved to be one of the busiest we had experienced with the business. Joe was always on the go, and I was constantly on the phone with bookings and checking in tour groups on a daily basis. When we first arrived home from Cabo, Joe had been affectionate and loving. He even told me that he was so happy that I was his wife. I loved hearing that. I was happy for a short time, but it didn't last long.

One day, Joe came home and said that he wanted to expand his business to another location. He wanted to find a town where he wouldn't have any competition and that had a high record of tourists visiting the area. I thought it was a great idea until he said, "That means we would have to find a place to live there and sell this house." "What? I thought you were just talking about getting someone to run the business for you at another location. You're talking about moving? What about the kids? They could be pulled out of school and Christy won't let you take Hannah, which means you would hardly ever see her."

I could tell he had started to become angry because I had questioned his idea. "You just don't get it, Renee. This business is what puts food on the table and a roof over our heads. The tour business here is oversaturated, and it's getting harder and harder to get bookings. Other competitors are now low balling their rates, and I won't be able to operate the business at those prices. I can't compete with that, and if the business goes under, then I'll be working somewhere like Home Depot."

What are you talking about, Joe? I handle your financials, and the business has brought in more money in these past few months then it did the previous summers."

"Renee, it's not going to stay that way. It will change, and I don't want to wait for that to happen. We need to have another location to help buffer what may happen eventually in this location. I'm only thinking of you and the kids. You're my family."

How could I argue with him? What if the business did eventually suffer? I just didn't see it but maybe he was right. I started to think about a fresh start. The house we were currently living in was the house he had shared with Christy. Maybe it was time for us to start a new life together somewhere else. A place where no one knew us. We would make new friends, have new neighbors, and find a location where the business would thrive, but where?

I would have to talk to Samuel. He had recently moved closer to the kids, and I felt terrible telling him that we may move to another city or state. I wondered how that was going to go, not to mention that Joe may have a fight on his hands with Christy, who currently lived two blocks away. I knew she wouldn't allow Hannah to move with us. From what I had gathered, she didn't trust Joe with Hannah, and she was well aware of his violent outbursts.

At the time, I thought there would be a slim chance of us moving since we would have to find the perfect location and that could prove hard to do, so I brushed it off, thinking it was just one of Joe's outlandish ideas. Over the next month, Joe traveled to various locations, exploring areas with stable weather conditions for his tour operation. He asked that I accompany him on his next trip out of state to Newberg, Oregon.

I thought it would be a nice little getaway for just the two of us. I was surprised to learn that Newberg was a charming little town and a high tourist area due to the countless rivers and forests offering boating, fishing, and hunting opportunities. It was a beautiful area, surrounded by rolling hills and several golf courses, and the moderate climate made it perfect for booking group tours year-round.

Additionally, it was also known for its world-class wine tasting, which holds a reputation of being the Napa Valley of Oregon. The small-town spirit had a relaxed pace that complimented the friendly people that lived there. The historic downtown area was full of quaint eateries and amazing wine tasting rooms. Best of all, the schools were top-rated in the area. I could see our family living there, and for the first time, I began to feel excited about a possible move.

Joe liked it because of the tourism it brought in. It was ideal since most of the tourists came from all over the world. I had always wanted to live in a small town since all I had ever known was the big city lifestyle. This area was a perfect place for families. The people were friendly, and I loved the historic charm of the town. I immediately began to research house rentals in the area. We would need to see if the business could succeed there and if everything fell into place, then we could look at eventually purchasing a home.

There weren't a lot of rentals on the market at the time, but the last one we looked at was nestled in a tree-lined neighborhood with breathtaking views, overlooking the valley. It wouldn't be available until the beginning of December, which would give us enough time to find renters for our current home. Within a week, we heard back from the owners of the house in Newberg. They liked the fact that we had children and offered the rental to us on the spot over the other applicants.

This was really happening! We would be moving in a month and a half. This also meant registering the kids in a new school. I was overwhelmed by it all. After speaking to Emma and Ryan and my ex-husband, we decided that Ryan would finish his senior year of high school where he was, so he decided to live with his father.

Emma would be moving with me. A piece of me felt terrible for ripping the kids apart, and I could tell that Emma wasn't happy about it. I couldn't bear to lose her too. She was just starting high school, so I was hoping the transition wouldn't be as hard for her. Things would most likely be difficult at first, but I believed it would be a better quality of life for us all and the fresh start would do everyone good. I held on to that in my heart. I had to. Samuel even offered to fly Emma to Phoenix whenever she wanted, so they could see each other as much as possible. I was happy that we were able to sort out the details together, but it still hurt me that I wouldn't see Ryan much.

He was now working at a local grocery store and saving money to take flight lessons, in hopes of getting his private pilot's license. He had loved planes since he was a little boy, and the calling to become a pilot had always been within him. I was happy for him and yet, still felt sad to leave him. At least we didn't have to worry about Callie since Joe had sole custody of her. I waited for the psychological mind games that would ensue between Joe and Christy and how they would divide their time with Hannah.

I could hear Joe on the phone, his voice becoming louder and angrier as he tried his hardest to make his point with Christy. "This will be a better lifestyle for Hannah! It's a small town with a better school district, and Hannah will have Callie and Emma around. She won't be all alone! She needs to get away from the bad influence of friends she's around now, and she needs to work on pulling up her grades. She will have a better quality of life that can prepare her for the future."

That was all Christy had to hear as if Joe had just told her she was a bad mother. She refused to let Hannah leave and tried to convince him to stay in the area until Hannah was older as she was not going to allow Hannah to move with us. "Fine, that's your choice, Christy! Hannah will suffer because you're making the wrong decision! I'm not paying you anymore in child support either since I already pay you enough every month!" I shuddered at the thought of them going through another court battle, and I prayed that wouldn't happen.

Joe came storming out of the room. "She's a fu***** bitch!" We've been getting along fine, and now with this move, she can't even see what's in Hannah's best interest!" "Joe, she's her mother. She doesn't want to lose her daughter. No court of law is going to choose you over Christy unless you could prove Hannah's in an unstable and dangerous environment, and she's not."

I was used to these situations. Everything had to be the way Joe saw it. It was his way or no way at all. There was no convincing him of anything. He would have to accept that Hannah would not be moving with us and would have to work out a schedule to see her with Christy. That's all he could do, and he knew it. I tried to keep him calm by telling him I understood. He continued his angry rant. My body trembled with fear, paralyzed with his malicious words that followed.

"I should just convince her to come to see the town and the schools. I'd like to take her out to a deserted area far out in the hills and kill her with my gun, then Hannah could come and live with us!"

"Joe, that's a terrible thing to say! You don't mean that!" I couldn't believe he would actually say something so horrific. I had been with Joe long enough to know that he had a spiteful way of saying things to get a reaction out of people, so of course, I never believed he would do such a thing, but to hear him say it out loud, and the fact that he had a gun in a locked safe turned my stomach.

"All she's ever done is make my life miserable! She's tried to take everything from me and now she wants to keep Hannah from having a better life! You're lucky because your ex just agrees with everything you guys discuss. You never have to go through what I have to! You don't understand!" I suddenly went on the defensive. I was sure as hell not going to apologize to Joe because Samuel and I got along like mature adults and were able to talk things through when it came to our children.

Before I could say anything in defense, his phone rang. I remained silent as he took the call and walked out the door. I heard his truck back out of the driveway. What the hell had just happened? I was left standing there once again trying to figure it all out. I went to bed that night waiting for him to come home. I was angry that he had left but somehow relieved as he walked back in the door, hoping he would have calmed down by now. Where had he gone? He crawled into bed and curled up next to me as I felt his arm pull me in tightly to him.

"Are you okay, Joe? Where did you go?"

"I just needed to deal with this myself. No one understands how terrible Christy is. She's so vindictive. I tried talking to my father, and he told me he's tired of hearing about it. I just feel so alone."

I noticed Joe hadn't told me where he had gone, and he was trying to change the subject, wanting me to feel sorry for him. All I could feel was anger. After standing by and supporting this man through all that I had, how could he tell me he felt so alone? What was I to him? His own father had finally put his foot down and told him he didn't want to hear any more about it. If I did that, boy, it would have escalated into one of his violent tangents. I didn't like the fact that he kept telling me that I didn't understand. It was hurtful.

In fact, I believed Hannah needed to stay with her mother. Christy was a caring, nurturing person from what I could tell, and Hannah still needed her. I had tried mentioning that to Joe once, and he was infuriated that I would even say such a thing. His response to my thoughts on the matter was, "You just want Hannah to stay with Christy so you don't have to deal with her. It would be one less kid you would have to worry about. I know you never wanted her to move with us."

I was so offended. "How dare you say such a thing to me! That is so wrong! You know that's not true! I love Hannah and she and Emma are really close, plus Callie looks up to her too. It would be much easier if everyone stayed together, but Christy is her mother. You are not the only parent here. You owe me an apology!" I could tell he was surprised by my reply.

"Renee, I didn't say that you didn't want Hannah to move with us."

"What? You just said it, Joe!"

"I never said that! You're crazy! You misunderstood what I said!"

I didn't know it then, but he was gaslighting me. He would frequently tell me that my version of events or a conversation was wrong, and it often made me question my own sanity. He would use this manipulative tactic to say something, then deny he ever said it or that I heard it wrong.

This was a dangerous mind game, and I was often left questioning my reality. I was naïve to all of this, which usually ended up leaving me foggy and confused. At that time, I didn't know anything about personality disorders. I always thought that dangerous people would be easy to spot, but he wasn't. He could make someone believe his lies were the truth by his glibness and superficial charm. This was emotional abuse, and it was sickening.

"Joe, I think you need to speak to a behavioral therapist. You need help learning to control and channel your anger. Maybe talking to someone would really help you." I didn't want to tell him the rest of what I was thinking which would have been, *"Someone needs to help you stop blaming everyone for your own mistakes, the choices you make, and the lies you tell,"* but of course, I didn't say that.

"I don't need help, Renee! I've been to counseling in the past, and I already know what's wrong with me!" I was surprised this had never surfaced in conversation before. There were things I didn't know about Joe and things I probably never would. "Well, please explain it to me then." I waited for a crazy concocted story but none came. He never replied and walked out the door looking mad as hell. I never got my answer.

For the next few days, I received the silent treatment, which I believed, was a way for him to avoid the subject from where it had been left, as well as avoiding having to apologize to me. I wasn't surprised. He had rarely ever apologized for anything, and, sadly, I grew accustomed to his sadistic abuse. Now that I know the traits and characteristics of a sociopath, I know that they find it nearly impossible to admit they're ever wrong. They will always, and I mean always, find a way to turn it around on the other person, and Joe did.

I concentrated my efforts on finding tenants to lease our house. It didn't take long. I found a nice, responsible couple to secure a year's lease, just in time for our move to Newberg. It felt strange packing our belongings, and a piece of my heart was broken having to say goodbye to Ryan, but a part of me also felt better about him living with his father.

He needed his father, who had always been there for him. He wouldn't have to endure listening to Joe's wild outbursts and evil temper tantrums. Joe had never really acted like a stepfather that I wish he could have been to Ryan, but Ryan had an inner strength in him that I believed came from God. I just felt it, and I knew he would be okay. It didn't make it any easier saying goodbye to my firstborn, who was now seventeen and almost an adult himself. I couldn't hide the tears that followed. As if reading my mind, he hugged me for the last time. "I'll be okay, mom."

I watched Emma hug Ryan goodbye and they giggled. They had silly nicknames for each other. Emma chuckled, "Bye, Mr. Weenie. We had called our little dog that, and that dog had loved Ryan. He walked away, laughing, "Bye, Stuie." That name somehow had stuck with them over the years from the television show, *Family Guy*. It sounded silly, but it was cute to see them interact that way as brother and sister. They loved each other, and it hurt knowing they wouldn't be seeing as much of one another.

We all went over to say our goodbyes to Hannah as well. She surprisingly didn't look upset as I thought it probably hadn't hit her yet that we would be so far away. Thankfully, Christy had finally agreed to allow Hannah to come up over the summer months and stay with us while she was out of school as well as some of the longer holiday breaks.

I thought it was fair, but Joe still argued the fact that it wasn't. He wanted Hannah to move in with us full time, so he continued to drill Christy on how exceptional the school districts were in the area, including a list of all of the advantages that small-town living offered. However, Christy wouldn't budge. Hannah would stay with her over the school year, and she wouldn't discuss it further. It took some time for Joe to accept that Hannah would only be living with us for a few months over the summer each year. I only hoped this move would be the fresh start I had prayed for.

Chapter Eighteen

Things Aren't Always as they Seem

It had been only a month since we had moved in. Emma and Callie were adjusting to their new schools. The students in Callie's class seemed to have given her a warm welcome and made her feel comfortable from the start. Emma's experience was quite different since she was just entering high school and didn't know anyone. I had prayed that the kids there would be nicer than most in a big city school. She had been quiet lately, and I could tell she was missing her father, Ryan, and Hannah.

One day, as I pulled into the school parking lot, I could see she was talking to someone. As she opened the car door, a girl shouted, "Bye, Emma, we love you!" It was nice to hear, and it seemed that Emma was making friends.

"Wow, Emma! That was sweet. Is she a new friend of yours?"

"Yeah, kind of mom. She's nice."

That made me feel good, but I still detected that something was off.

"What's the matter, Emma? I can tell something is wrong."

"Nothing mom, I'm fine. It's just a lot at once to adjust to, and I also miss riding horses."

"Oh, well, maybe we can see if anyone offers riding lessons close by. I mean, we're in the country out here so there has to be something."

"That would be fun, but I don't think I want to take lessons. I just want to ride for pleasure. Maybe there's someone out here that would allow me to ride their horse for exercise."

"I'm not sure about that, Emma, because that could be a liability for them. We will see, okay?"

"Okay, mom."

As I glanced over at her, I could see her face light up with the thought. She missed riding and the special bond she had with horses. Later that evening, I asked Joe if he knew anyone that had horses that would allow Emma to go along on a trail ride with them. "No, I don't know anyone who would do that, but I have been thinking about getting a few horses for a trail-riding business. We could run it on the weekends and then Emma could ride them whenever she wanted to. They will need the exercise anyways if they are boarded at a barn."

My heart skipped a beat. I couldn't wait to tell Emma. I could even ride with her as I had grown up riding horses and suddenly thought it would be a great way to spend time together with Emma. But just as I was going to talk to her about it, Joe said, "I think we should surprise Emma with a horse. She's helped us a lot with Callie, she gets good grades and has stayed out of trouble, so she deserves it. We should look for a horse first, and if you like it, we will have Emma ride it, then bring the horse to wherever we end up boarding it."

I couldn't believe it! Joe wanted to do something nice for my daughter. He had never done anything like this. Was there a method to his kindness? Was he going to throw his grandiose view of himself back in my face every time he did something deceitful or that he knew I would disapprove of? I was willing to take the risk for Emma's happiness. I wanted her to love it here. Owning our very own horses would be a dream come true. I wasn't exactly sure if a trail-ride business would be ideal due to the cost and legalities of obtaining equine insurance, but I knew that was the only way Joe would consider having our own horses. At the end of the day, it came down to business.

The Mercedes I had no longer was practical where we now lived, so Joe had recently traded it in for a pre-owned Lincoln SUV. He would always say, "Only the best for my wife." It was nice, and I actually enjoyed driving the kids around in it. It was a dependable vehicle and suited us for our new lifestyle. Joe had a way of making me feel special with the things he would buy me, but I knew him well enough to know there would come a time that he would make me feel guilty for having it. He liked to dominate me in these situations. Making me feel special at first but then turning it around telling me what he had done for me as if I didn't appreciate it. I would be made to feel so guilty that it would completely break me down, and usually, I would end up in my quiet place, sitting on the floor of my bathroom, crying.

I was either ignored and given the silent treatment for days or he would buy me something else, and the vicious cycle would start all over again. I was used to this by now. It had become my way of life, but I was determined to make my marriage work. A part of me still believed this man loved me, no matter what actions he took. He had a sickness, and at times I would pray that he would get help for his behavior.

We decided to purchase three horses for our trail-ride business and surprised Emma one day by asking her if she wanted to ride a beautiful bay gelding. She had thought we were going to just look at horses, but when she started to ride the bay and told us how much she loved him, we told her we were taking him to a boarding facility close to home and she would be responsible for taking care of him. He was her horse. The look on her face brought tears to my eyes. Crying, she thanked Joe with a hug. I was overjoyed seeing how happy she was.

Within the next month, we had purchased the other two horses. I had never seen Emma so content and happy. Even Callie seemed to like the interaction with the horses and enjoyed being at the barn. Emma's mood had changed. One day at the barn, she told me, "I'm so glad we moved out here, mom. I never thought we would own our own horses." I couldn't help but ask her, "What will you do when you start getting interested in boys and wanting to date? Are you still going to give the horses your attention?"

She looked at me as if I should have known the answer. She loved all the horses, especially the one named Kensington. "I don't need any boyfriends, mom. I have Kensington." All I could think was, *"Hallelujah! Thank you, Lord!"* Life was good for a short while until Joe became angry that he couldn't obtain liability insurance. No insurance company would accept his application for equine insurance since he was just starting the business. The cost of boarding three horses started to become an issue I would hear about daily.

This had been his idea and now I felt like it had become my problem. I was fearful that he might tell me that we would have to sell the horses, telling me he couldn't afford the board and vet checks; however, I knew he could as he spent lavish amounts of money on other non-related work projects that suited him. I was supportive of his choices since I knew that financially he could afford it, but I also knew he wasn't breaking the bank if we had horses.

Every once in a while, he would go on a trail ride with Emma and me, which was nice. He could ride, but he hadn't grown up around horses or taken lessons like Emma and I had. He had more of a cowboy mentality, thinking he was superior to our style of riding and what he thought was best. One day he insisted on taking Kensington out on a trail ride when my mother came to visit. I was against it. He had put the wrong kind of saddle on Kensington, and he wouldn't take my advice and turn him out to run in the arena after days of not being exercised. Kensington was the kind of horse that needed to be constantly worked, and my daughter was visibly shaken by Joe's know it all attitude.

Even a trainer that boarded her horse at the barn tried to politely show Joe how to position the saddle and cinch so it wouldn't pinch Kensington while riding. Joe didn't have the gentlest hands either, as we were nervous that he might be too hard on Kensington's mouth when reining him. Joe, of course, insisted he was fine, and once the trainer left, I heard him say, "No woman is going to tell me what to do!" He wouldn't even take her suggestion, and he didn't want to be outshined by a woman. I had to say something. "Joe, she was only trying to help you and was concerned for your safety and Kensington's." He continued cinching his saddle as if I wasn't there, then chided, "She's crazy! I know what I'm doing!" The end result was catastrophic.

Once they left for their ride, I had an overwhelming sense that something wasn't right. As I was waiting for my mother and Joe to return, my phone rang. It was Joe, and I was shocked to hear him crying. My heart sank.

"Renee, get up here on the trail now! Kensington is gone!"

"Joe, what are you talking about? What do you mean he's gone?"

I started to panic, looking for the barn manager, hoping he could take me quickly in his four-wheeler to the trail they had taken. I listened to Joe's story in disbelief. Kensington had spooked and reared with him. Joe had been so scared that he slid off the saddle and let go of the reins. Kensington had galloped off, and he wasn't sure where he had gone. As I started making my way to the trail, I saw Joe walking down the trail with Kensington. I froze in a state of shock at the sight of our beautiful horse. Half of the skin on his face had been torn off and his back leg had a huge gash in it. He could barely walk.

My adrenaline must have kicked in. As I called the vet with one hand and took the reins from Joe in the other, I walked back to the barn with Kensington, trying to console him. We ran cold water over his body to keep him from going into shock until the vet arrived. I honestly couldn't believe he was standing. I felt sick, and Emma was crying at the sight of her best friend in such a terrible condition. The vet rushed him off to a clinic where he had to undergo facial reconstructive surgery. He was under constant supervision for two weeks. Thankfully, he started to heal, and he showed no signs of lameness. Five thousand dollars later, he was well enough to come home but would need stall rest for another two months, following continual monitoring of his right eye. They informed us there was a chance he would be blind in that eye, as only time would tell if it had been permanently damaged.

How could this have happened? The only thing that made sense was that Kensington had tripped over something on the ground and had been hit by a low-lying branch of a tree, resulting in his facial injuries. Why would Joe let go of the reins? Why didn't he take the trainer's advice about the saddle and why wouldn't he have exercised him first? I was mad at him for his *"I know everything attitude,"* but he learned an expensive lesson that day.

A five-thousand-dollar one, to be exact. I could tell he knew he had acted wrong, but I also knew he would never admit it. I'm not even sure if his crying had been genuine. He did come with me though to visit Kensington when he was recovering in the clinic. A part of me wanted to believe he felt terrible for putting Kensington through such an ordeal; however, I was ready to stand up to him if he tried to ride him again, no matter what he said or did.

Eventually, Kensington healed, and my daughter rode him as if no time had passed between them. They had such a special bond, and it was heartfelt to see them together again. The vet had given us a green light for short rides, and by the grace of God, he made a full recovery—no blindness, no lameness, nothing. We were even told that his recovery was miraculous as some horses weren't so lucky. Joe came into the barn soon after to see how Kensington had recovered. I couldn't shake the strange vibe that now hung in the air when he was there.

Emma and I had become friends with a nice couple at the barn, and we all enjoyed going on trail rides together. I wanted to introduce them to Joe as they had never met in person. "Joe, this is Jean and Dan, my friends that I go on trail rides with." Dan extended his hand. "Nice to meet you, Joe." Joe continued to groom one of our other horses and didn't even approach Dan to offer a handshake in return. Instead, he decided to ridicule me in front of my friends.

"I'm the husband, the guy who pays for everything, the guy who makes it possible to have these horses." I was stunned by his arrogant response. Jean and Dan looked on shockingly and walked back to their horses in the pasture. "Joe, that was so rude! You could have said nice to meet you or at least shake Dan's hand in return. Why did you have to act that way?"

"What are you talking about, Renee? It's the truth! These horses are costing me a small fortune, and I do pay for everything so you and Emma can ride. You don't even appreciate what I do for you."

"What? How could you even say that? I say thank you all the time, and the only reason you got these horses in the first place is because you wanted to run a business with them but now need someone to blame since it didn't pan out. That's not my fault, and by the way, let me remind you that you said you wanted to get Emma a horse as a reward for getting good grades and for how much she has helped with Callie!"

I was ready to go in a corner and cry. He showed a total disregard for my feelings. I stormed off to the bathroom to regain my composure and went to apologize to Jean and Dan for Joe's rude behavior before leaving that day. I could tell by the way Jean looked at me that she had felt sorry for me. I had been humiliated once again. I thought things had possibly changed with our move here, but I was quickly reminded that things aren't always as they seem. Maybe it was just what I wanted to see.

Chapter Nineteen

The Rose-Colored Glasses Effect

I had made every possible effort to see Joe in a more positive light. I had tried many times to see him through rose-colored glasses. He had been so kind and giving in the last few months. I thought things would be different starting over somewhere new and living in a small town would allow us to spend more time together. Most of the restaurants and tasting rooms in the neighborhood closed early, so he wouldn't have the opportunity to stay out late at night as he had before. At least, that's what I believed.

Once Ryan came to visit over spring break, Joe thought he would like to go up on a helicopter tour at the local airport. Ryan, of course, was excited to go. Christy had allowed Hannah to also visit over the two weeks she was out of school. It felt wonderful to spend time together as a family again. Joe seemed to be in a good mood and was lost in conversation with two of the men in the heliport office. I could tell he was curious about the business operation after he met Brad, the owner of the company.

Brad's wife, Tina, was a joy to talk to. She was the first woman I had met that I really felt a connection to. I could see us becoming fast friends. She also had a daughter that was Emma's age, and we found that we had a lot in common with each other. She had even moved here from Utah to start a new life with Brad. The man standing next to Brad seemed to know a great deal about helicopters, and Joe was soaking up his every word like a sponge. I could tell that he was transfixed by this man. His name was Shane.

I thought Shane was nice at first. He was funny, intelligent, and an all-around nice guy. He was about Joe's age, and I could see them becoming friends. However, unbeknownst to me, Joe becoming friends with Shane would soon lead to the downfall of our marriage. Soon, we were invited to Shane's house for a pool party. I enjoyed the warm conversation about our recent move there with his wife, Sarah, who seemed kind and sincere.

The kids enjoyed splashing each other and playing in the pool as it was a welcome relief to some of the warmer days. Joe started having a guy's night out with Shane, which I understood, but it became more and more frequent, as much as four to five nights a week. I knew if I had spent that much time with a friend, Joe would have read me the riot act on not being there for the family, so I finally asked him why he needed to go to Shane's house all the time. At least, that's where I thought he was.

I was told that he and Shane liked *hanging out* together and that I should mind my own business. "I can go out anytime I want! Quit being so insecure, Renee! Shane has become a good friend, and if I want to go to his house and have a beer, then I will! Get over it!" Something in me soured at that very moment. Maybe their friendship was something I didn't understand. What man spends so much time with another man, instead of being home with his family? The guilt he laid on me from just asking him made me feel that maybe I was being insecure, but in my heart, I still felt something was off.

Having a beer with Shane meant that he would be gone until late at night. It really was no different than what he had been doing before. Hannah had even mentioned that when she had come to visit, questioning why I was always there at the house and Joe wasn't. Joe, of course, went off the deep end, telling her that she was lucky to have everything she did and that she saw him plenty and he didn't need to be at home when everyone was in bed. I felt bad for her. He didn't see how much it affected her when he wasn't home.

He always had an excuse—always. Callie had noticed it too, and when he had come home one day throwing one of his tantrums, she decided to tell him what she thought. "You're just mean, dad! Why do you always have to yell at mama?" I was mortified as he walked out to his car, shouting obscenities and threatening her with time-out in her room until further notice.

You could hear her wailing through her open window for having to stay in her room. She repeatedly screamed, "I hate you!" You're mean!" He raced back in the house. "You better shut up, Callie, or I'll give you something to really cry about!" I didn't know what to do and wondered if our neighbors had heard her cries and his wild outbursts. Waving his arms wildly as he came towards me, the words that followed sent a shiver down my spine.

"God damn kids! I never wanted that kid! My life would be so different if I didn't have her! I'm ready to send her back to her grandparents in Texas!"

I couldn't believe it! I stood there, frozen in shock, as he became silent. Callie's window was open, and I believed she had heard everything he said. An overwhelming sense of fear washed over me. How could he say something so cruel? That was pure evil. I was also struck by the fact that he said *"his life"* would have been different, not *"our life."* Everything was about him and what he wanted. We were all just puppets being controlled and manipulated by him. Who was this man? I had never heard him say such callous things about his own children, but he wasn't finished. "Hannah better get her act together too!"

She had been doing poorly in school and had recently been caught with a vape pen, which resulted in a suspension for two days. He pressed Christy even more at the time to have Hannah come and live with us. Christy was pondering the idea of letting Hannah live with us for a school year, but nothing had been decided yet. "Why is my kid such a screw-up? She's going to end up being a loser like her mother! She's never going to amount to anything! She'll end up working for me when she gets older!"

My head was spinning. Why would he say these things? I worked for him too, so did that mean he thought I was a loser as well? He loved Hannah, and I didn't know why he would say so many vicious things about her. "Joe, the things you just said about Callie and Hannah are terrible! They're your children! You're just angry at everyone and don't even mean what you just said!"

I could still hear Callie's cries and walked back in the house, unable to even look at him without feeling a stabbing pain stirring inside of me. I went into Callie's room to see Emma consoling her with a gentle hug, telling her it would be okay. I loved that Emma had such a giving nature and the selflessness that she showed to others, especially when it came to Callie. Callie called her "*sissy.*" She looked up to her, and I was happy she could be there for her.

Whether it had been a tinge of guilt, anger, or both, Joe had driven off, never telling me where he was going or when he would be back. This new start for us here had not been what I imagined. Nothing ever was anymore. Instead of thinking of the opportunity we may have had growing closer together, I regrettably only felt the effects of us growing further and further apart. Did he even want a family?

Chapter Twenty

Inseparable

At times, Joe made it seem like he was really being selfless, but now I know that deep down inside, he was already planning exactly how he was going to twist it around for his own benefit. I had heard it all before, whether he was stressed out from getting the business off the ground here, how he had wished he didn't have to pay Christy child support, or even fantasizing about the money that Shane had made in his advertising business. Everything Shane did or said, Joe wanted to be a part of it.

Of course, Joe could never take the blame for anything but instead would dump all of his negative views on me, always ranting about his problems and how unfair the world was and always blaming other people for what was going wrong in life. If I tried to offer advice or help him, he normally didn't want to hear what I thought, only what Shane did. Apparently, I never understood. That was his favorite thing to say, "*You just don't understand, Renee!*" I was just there to listen and endure it all as his emotional punching bag.

If I caught him being rude or insulting at times, he would brush it off and say, *"Just kidding,"* even though there was nothing funny about it. It was his way of gaining the attention he sadistically craved. He found a cruel pleasure in being mean, always finding ways to mentally or emotionally hurt me, which in turn, gave him more power and control over me. His need to be right all the time was overbearing, and if I didn't agree or had a difference of opinion, I would eventually either be forced to agree with him or rudely silenced.

Joe had a way of considering his own opinions as facts and would criticize or even laugh at anyone that opposed his views. He always believed his method or way of doing things was the best and the only way because it guaranteed his needs were met, and that's all that really mattered to him. He had taken advantage of my emotional sensitivity and sympathy.

All I had ever wanted to do was help him, love him, and support him, and he abused that kindness to reel me in to help him get what he wanted. I was finding it difficult to even trust myself. He had worn me down, and I was tired. I started to agree with everything he would say, and I stopped questioning him, even when he blatantly lied to me. I had become confused and disoriented and found there was no one left around me that I could trust but my children.

On one particular day, completely out of the blue, he informed me that he and Shane had been preparing for a trip together to New Zealand. They were planning on taking a flight instruction course over the majestic scenery that offered views of the Southern Alps. He couldn't resist going somewhere with someone that was now a big part of his life and who he had so much in common with. I was happy for him but at the same time, I had been trying to plan a trip for us to just get away for a weekend together, and he had said he couldn't shut down the business.

He made time for what was important to him and anytime that I wanted to go out on a date night, I was met with, "I'll call Shane and see what he's doing. He and Sarah should come too." I made several attempts trying to tell him that it would be nice if it was just the two of us on a date but then he would become angry and ask me why I didn't like Shane. Shane was all I heard about or how great Shane's kids were.

Shane's wife, Sarah, was a family attorney and did very well for herself. Joe enjoyed boasting about her around me, which left me feeling constantly humiliated and beaten down. I wondered if he even realized that he wouldn't have been where he was in his business if it wasn't for me or even be able to go out every night and enjoy his freedom with his newfound friend.

I had done the math, and if Joe would have paid someone monthly to do all the things that I did for him, he would have had to pay at least five-thousand dollars a month, and I wasn't even taking a salary or receiving any kind of pay. If I brought it up to him, he would just tell me that I had a roof over my head and food on the table. I just wanted to feel appreciated. I just wanted to feel like enough. I just wanted to feel like me again.

Since he was still operating the business in Phoenix, he decided to advertise with the event venue at the local fairgrounds. I thought he would ask me to go with him since we had been planning the event schedule for the past month, but instead, he asked Shane to go with him. Joe knew I was disappointed and hurt by him taking Shane instead of me, knowing that I had wanted to go, but he reasoned that this was just business, and someone had to take care of the kids.

Joe had trained me over time to become afraid of doing the very things that once made my life fulfilling. If there was anything that threatened the control he held over me, he would seek to destroy it. No one ever questioned him, but of course, everyone else only saw the charming, charismatic Joe, not the man I lived with. I was like his puppet, tethered toxically to him, and he controlled me through my emotions.

I had started drinking heavily again, mainly to numb myself from the pain I felt, but also from the sheer loneliness and feelings of being unwanted by a man that had once told me that I was his everything. A man that wanted to be with me. A man that would have given me the world. That man never really existed. Joe was a skilled actor whose sole mission was to manipulate me for his personal gain and to get me to do whatever he wanted.

He called me on the first night he was at the fairgrounds with Shane. He sounded happy that his marketing efforts were going well and was surprised by how many people had inquired about booking a tour. We mainly talked about business as I told him how busy the phones had been. He abruptly cut me off stating he had to go and should be finishing up at the fairgrounds shortly. I was still overly bitter about Shane going with him as Shane didn't know the business as I did but my heart told me what I already knew.

He just wanted to have his freedom to do whatever it was he was doing, and I'm sure Shane would have his back if anyone ever questioned him about it. Of course, that *anyone* would be me. Lately, everything was about Shane. He went to lunch with Shane, he went to have beers with Shane, he went to Shane's office to learn his business, he went to Shane's house most weekends, sometimes bringing the kids so they could go swimming. If he agreed to a date night, Shane would suddenly show up with his wife. When he was home, he was indifferent as if he wasn't really there, always saying he had something to do in the garage or tackling a new home project.

I kept asking myself, *"Why did Joe feel the need to spend so much time with Shane, and why couldn't we just go somewhere together, just he and I?"* Something just didn't feel right about it. My health started to deteriorate.

At my last doctor's appointment, the doctor had told me my blood pressure had been high and asked if I was under a lot of stress. I had never had high blood pressure in my life but a part of me knew this was my life now, and I couldn't do anything to change it unless I left him, but I couldn't abandon Callie and I couldn't leave Joe. I didn't know how to live without him. Divorce was not an option.

Once he arrived back home, he kept himself busy as usual. I noticed he had left his phone behind one day as he left to run errands. Something inside me told me that I needed to look at his phone, but I was scared that I might find something that I didn't want to find. Still, it was an opportunity to know if my intuition was right. I didn't want to be right. I looked out the window making sure he hadn't returned. His phone wasn't password-protected, so I quickly scanned his texts and saw one from him to Shane that said,

"Where are you? Hurry up and get back here. I can't handle all three of them by myself." What the hell? Was he talking about three women? My hands started to shake at what I saw next in a photo. Joe was surrounded by three pretty blonde women who looked to be triplets, provocatively dressed in leather mini-skirts and knee-high boots. One of them had their tanned leg wrapped around Joe's body, exposing her braless chest through her sheer blouse. The woman on the other side of Joe was kissing his cheek, her body pressing tightly against his. There he was,

right in the middle of it all, with the biggest smile on his face.

I started to cry as I threw his phone across the room. Why did he marry me? It had become obvious to me that he liked living like he was single. It made me sick to my stomach to think about what he had been doing. I picked up his phone and placed it back on the bed, looking at the photo once more. I couldn't compete with these women, nor did I want to. My gut feeling had been right.

I tried to act as normal as I could that night as we all went out for pizza. Joe was in a good mood and chatting with the kids. Emma could sense my contemptuous vibe as I was short with Joe with anything he had to say. "Why are you being that way, mom?" I couldn't very well tell her what I had found, but I was so desperate for someone to talk to. All I could think of in a disconcerting response is what Joe had said to me time and time again. "What way? I don't know what you're talking about." I knew that my daughter could tell something was off, which was enough for her to know not to press me about it further.

Joe had waited to ask me what was wrong once the kids had gone to bed. "I can tell something is bothering you, Renee." I could no longer hold in my anger and overwrought emotions from what I had found on his phone. "Oh, like you care if something is bothering me." I was shaking and finding it difficult to control the tears that were starting to flow.

"Of course I care, Renee. I love you."

"Really? Is that what you told the blonde triplets at the event too? Do you love them as well?"

The look of concern on Joe's face suddenly turned to fear and frustration. "You're crazy, Renee! What are you talking about?" Have you been drinking? You're acting like a jealous drunk. He wanted me to say it, and I wasn't going to let him twist it around and turn it on me. "I saw the photos on your phone, and I read what you said to Shane. You can't lie your way out of it this time!" I had called him out on it, and I didn't know what story he could possibly try to make up.

"Those were the Jack Daniels girls. Didn't you see the drinks in their hands? All I did was take a photo with them, and I was just joking around with Shane. I didn't cheat on you, Renee!" It was interesting that I hadn't asked him if he had cheated on me outright, but he made sure to tell me that he hadn't. "Why are you going through my phone? You don't trust me?"

"You didn't want me to go to the event with you and now I know why you didn't! Anything you ever want to do is with Shane and not me. What if the tables were turned, Joe? What if I had been the one with three hunky men that had their bodies pressed against me with one of them kissing me? How would you feel if you saw a photo of that on my phone?"

What he said next was an outright lie. "I would trust you, Renee. The problem is that you don't trust me. I have never cheated on you, nor will I ever cheat on you. I might look at other women but all men do. You are the only one I want to be with, and I wish you would trust me when I'm hanging out with Shane." What the hell had just happened? I felt like I had just had the wind knocked out of me. He was a swift and skillful liar, and sometimes he was so disingenuous that his actions and facial expressions gave him away.

I even felt a strange sense that he wasn't even believing his own words, and yet, he was trying to convince me this was the truth. I knew he would have gone crazy had he seen a photo of me with other men posing like that. I was tired and disgusted with him, and I knew he would not back down from his fabricated story. "I don't know what else to say, Renee. You could even ask Shane if I did anything. He will tell you."

"Are you serious, Joe? Why would I ask your bosom buddy if you did anything? I'm not an idiot. You both play by your own bro code, and one wouldn't dare oust the other. I know Shane says terrible things about his wife, Sarah, too. I've heard you both talking. Just stop lying to me. I'm sick of it!" He was unbelievably calm, which is something I wasn't used to. "I'm sorry that you don't trust me, Renee," as he pretentiously walked away, grabbing his phone.

I could hear him whispering, "hello," as he closed the door leading to the garage. I'm sure he was calling Shane to tell him what had happened. Nothing was ever kept private between us. Maybe he wanted to make sure they both had their stories straight if Shane ever found himself talking to me. I felt lightheaded and nauseous over the thought as the vicious cycle of anxiety I knew all too well quickly returned.

Chapter Twenty-One
A Birthday Nightmare

I couldn't help the thoughts that came rushing to my mind, wondering why Joe would cheat on me. Was I not good enough? Was the marriage a cover-up to some secret fling he had on the side? Was he one of those men that just couldn't stay faithful to one woman? Or, was it as simple as he really didn't love me? After all, he had told me he never really loved his first wife.

It was the week of my birthday, and I didn't even want to be around him. He made reservations at a local restaurant and wine tasting room, but I still had not shaken my anxiety and wasn't feeling especially festive. I looked around, expecting to see Shane and Sarah there, but to my surprise, it was just the two of us. I couldn't remember the last time it was just him and I out together. As we experienced some of the fabulous wine selections, we discussed selling the house in Phoenix and purchasing a home in the valley close to town since the business was thriving.

Given that I still had my real estate license in Arizona, he wanted me to sell the house so I could obtain the commission from the sale with the goal of using the money towards the down payment of the purchase of a new home that would ultimately be ours together. I also agreed to represent him as a buyer's agent when we looked for homes in the area since we had discussed using the commission from that sale for restoring the property. Most of the homes in our area were outdated and would need a considerable amount of costly repairs.

It felt nice to get away from talking about Shane, although I wondered if he really wanted to buy a home here because of Shane. They were always joined at the hip, and I still couldn't shake the feeling that they had some shady secrets of their own that I would never know about. I could tell that Joe was aware of my lack of trust for him, and he knew that I had pulled further away.

He seemed to grow increasingly annoyed watching me try to force a smile and suddenly muttered, "You should be selling real estate on the side up here. I've spent hundreds of dollars trying to help you get your own business off the ground. There's no reason you can't. Look at Jenny, who's sold millions in home sales up here." Here I was, sitting with him and trying to enjoy a birthday dinner, and he had the audacity to try and humiliate and shame me in public.

"Jenny is a seasoned real estate broker in this valley that has been here over thirty-plus years. This is a small town and there's not a lot of homes for sale, and by the way, I have been busy running YOUR business and taking care of the kids, since you're always gone! Can we just talk about something else since it's my birthday?" I felt a sharp pain in my stomach as my anxiety rose to a new level. He looked at me as if he was ready for battle, and there was no way he was going to back down.

"No, you know me! I'm not going to change the subject. There's no reason you can't sell real estate on the side and do what Jenny does! Why can't you be just like Shane's wife and make ten grand a month?" Other people started to turn and stare shockingly in our direction as the callousness of his words permeated the room. I couldn't control my tears as I looked down at the floor and quickly ran to the bathroom, crying in the stall for what must have been more than ten minutes. I was tired of being made to feel I wasn't enough. What more did he want?

How could he compare me to Shane's wife or even a seasoned real estate broker that had lived here for thirty years? I felt sick with the thought that he only saw the money, and not me. Was he acting this way so he could take the pressure off himself with what he had done? I didn't even want to go to dinner in the first place, but he had insisted. Was this a show he was putting on, so he could ridicule me in front of everyone and somehow make himself feel better? Anything was possible now.

I tried my best to dry my eyes and walk back to the table, but judging by his body language and the scowl on his face for leaving him sitting there, I knew he wasn't finished, and I couldn't take any more of his constant insults and accusations. I would have lost control and broken down in tears, so I quickly went to the front door of the restaurant to call a taxi. I felt an overwhelming sense of dread as if I had made matters worse by trying to leave, but I just wanted to be far away from him and back at home with the kids, while somehow finding comfort in the belief that things would get better.

I couldn't believe this was happening. As I waited for the taxi, I saw Joe coming towards me in a fit of rage. "What the hell are you doing? I've been waiting for you at the table! You embarrassed the hell out of me! We're leaving! Get in the van!" I stood there, unsure of how to respond, but knew that he needed to calm down or I wasn't sure what he would do. "I'm not going anywhere with you, Joe! I'm taking a taxi home! Just leave me alone! You're making a scene."

I thought I had seen him at his worst, but he had blatantly proven me wrong. He stormed out the front door as he walked to his van, but then, he turned around and walked back inside, coming towards me and yanking my purse off my arm. He walked out the door with my purse in tow, screaming "Try taking a taxi now!" I was appalled at his cruel behavior, but my cell phone and wallet were in my purse, and I didn't have any other way home. I ran after him, pleading for him to give me my purse back.

He turned to face me with such rage, screaming "You're such a cunt! No one makes me look like a fool!"

He opened the side of the van door and threw my purse on the seat. "Go and get it, Renee!" He was fuming with uncontrollable anger as I reached in to grab my purse. I felt his arms come from behind me and push me inside the van onto the seat. We had taken his fifteen-passenger van we used to transport tour groups in since his truck was in the shop. I screamed as I tried to open the side sliding door to get out, but he wouldn't let me leave.

As I reached for my phone, he squeezed my hand so hard that I dropped it, and he shoved it in his pocket. I pleaded with him through my tears for him to give me the phone back as he pulled out of the parking lot and took the exit to the highway. Where were we going to? For a second, I thought this man could kill me, but then a part of me didn't believe he would. His scare tactics had always involved threats, but he never acted on them.

What if he was going to take me somewhere and kill me as he had said he wanted to do with his ex-wife? He surely seemed insane enough to do it at that moment. I had also never heard him call me a cunt. It was a new low, and I suddenly thought of Emma and Callie waiting for us to return from dinner. I needed to do something. I gathered what strength I had left and slid open the side door of the van. I could jump, but then what? I would surely be hurt by how fast he was speeding, but just then he slowed down, yelling at me to close the door. I refused as I pleaded with him for my phone.

"You want your phone?" Go get your fu***** phone!" I could hear myself screaming "No, please don't," as he threw it out the side of the van. I watched it fall through some trees, down into a ravine, as I pictured it shattering into a thousand pieces. It was gone. That phone was my only lifeline and all of my contacts had gone with it. I hadn't noticed another car that had been trailing us from behind, but the driver had seen me open my side door while the van was moving and thought he may have been witnessing a kidnapping. He pulled over and told Joe he was going to call the police unless he saw me get out of the van to make sure that I was alright.

Joe came over to me now with a calmer and concerned tone. "Renee, if you don't get out of the van to let this guy know you're alright, he's going to call the police." Oh, I thought about just sitting there as I wouldn't have minded if the police had shown up and questioned him on his wild behavior, but I knew I would make matters worse. I stepped out of the van and waved to the driver that I was okay. As he drove off, I glared at Joe, feeling angry and hurt.

"How could you do this to me? Why do you hate me so much, and why would you call me one of the worst names you could call a woman? I'm a good person and loyal and loving to you and the children. All you wanted to do was cause a fight and humiliate me in that restaurant. Why, Joe? Did it give you some sick satisfaction to throw my phone into a ravine? Where were you taking me anyway? I don't deserve this! It's my birthday, and one that I will remember as the worst birthday of my life!"

Much of what he had said was to just get a reaction out of me, and he succeeded. It was a sick game of manipulation he liked to play to gain more power over me. Sobbing and pouring out my emotions, I wanted answers to the questions about his evil behavior, wanting so badly to hear him apologize for the things he had said, but an apology from someone with no conscience was no apology at all.

"I'm sorry, Renee. I didn't mean to call you those names, and I don't hate you. I know I handled this evening wrong. I will make it up to you. I'll get you a new phone tomorrow. A better one. I'll take you away for your birthday somewhere, just you and me. Maybe we can go to Vegas."

"I don't want to go anywhere with you! You need help, Joe! Just take me home to the kids. I don't want to see you tonight! I just want peace and quiet for the rest of what's left of my birthday."

As he started to drive home with what I can only imagine was a sense of guilt for what he had done, I could hear him ordering a new phone for me. This was the second phone he had now purposely destroyed of mine. He slept on the couch that night, but I didn't sleep at all as I prayed for protection from the one man that I had loved, the same man who was hell-bent on destroying me.

Chapter Twenty-Two

Guess Who's Not Coming to Dinner?

My mother and stepfather came to visit two months later. Joe's outbursts and obscene behavior had taken a back seat since that terrible night. He never brought it up again. His way of mending our relationship included buying me the latest phone and by whisking me away on a weekend to Vegas full of shopping, sight-seeing, and shows. He was loving and attentive and made me feel as if he was truly sorry for the way he had acted, but a part of me couldn't help but feel it was short-lived and would only happen again.

It was a welcome relief to have my mother and stepfather there. We all enjoyed a few days of wine tasting at some of the top-rated wineries and tasting rooms. Joe turned up his charismatic charm around them both. I could tell that my stepfather, Richard, really took a liking to Joe, and for a while, I thought Joe was trying to convince them both to move up to the area. It felt good to feel a sense of normalcy for a change.

Joe had become friends with one of the owners at a local tasting room. Paul and his wife, Karen, were a well-known couple that produced exceptional wines locally in the valley. We thoroughly enjoyed our conversations with them, and Joe decided it would be nice if we had them over for dinner while my parents were still visiting.

We were expecting Paul and Karen for dinner at five o'clock. Joe had been running errands for most of the day and had not returned. It was now four-thirty. Where was he? I tried repeatedly calling him, but his phone only went to voicemail. I started to panic as he was the one that had said he would cook the dinner and yet, nothing had been done. I tried texting him and still no response. Why wouldn't he answer his phone?

My stepfather started to help me in the kitchen and ended up cooking most of the meal as Paul and Karen arrived. There was still no word from Joe. My fear started to turn to anger as I thought of what to say to Paul and Karen. They had both thought it was odd that Joe wasn't there, but we all decided to eat the wonderful dinner that Richard had so graciously made since the food was getting cold and no one knew what was going on. Paul was explaining his winemaking process to everyone when Joe casually walked in the door.

We all looked at him in disbelief and wanted to know what had happened to him. I struggled to understand his complete lack of disregard for not having the common decency to even be there. "Where have you been?" I've tried calling and texting you several times." He laughed, appearing to be slightly intoxicated. "I was at Shane's, and I lost track of time." That was it? That was his excuse? He was the one that invited Paul and Karen that evening and not showing up until dinner was over was even beneath him.

"Didn't you get any of my messages?" I wondered if he would be apologetic in front of Paul and Karen and my parents, but honestly, I believed he didn't care and felt no sense of guilt for being more than late to his own dinner party. "You could have called, Joe. We didn't know if something happened to you." Still laughing, he replied, "I didn't have my phone on me. It was in my van." I could sense that he was lying as his eyes glazed over. I knew how he was, even if I caught him in a lie, he would just create another lie to get away with as much as he could get away with. He was so convincing with others that he could get one to believe almost anything.

If that wasn't bad enough, sensing that Joe hadn't eaten, my stepfather started to get up from the table. "I'll go make you a plate," in which Joe quickly replied, "No, I don't need anything. I already ate pizza at Shane's." Silence filled the room as everyone sat frozen, startled by his ill-mannered remark. Joe just dismissed it as he had done nothing wrong while starting to drum up a conversation with Paul and Karen. Why had he eaten at

Shane's when he had invited his friends to have dinner with us, and why would he not even thank my stepfather for taking care of dinner?

I was the one left feeling embarrassed and discreetly apologized to my parents for his rude behavior. Why was I the one apologizing? I knew that if I had done the same thing to him with his father visiting, he would have accused me of being rude and disrespectful, which I'm sure would have resulted in one of his outlandishly evil rants. He had let his mask slip in front of me one too many times, exposing his lies, his deceptions, and his lack of empathy. No one saw this Joe. No one knew who he really was, but me.

Chapter Twenty-Three
Fool Me Twice

I had been given the silent treatment once again, which I believed was more for the reason of him not having to explain himself for his irrational behavior at the dinner party. Shane had been making more of an appearance lately at our house. I watched Joe as he eagerly planned his New Zealand trip with Shane on his computer, mapping out their flight paths, anticipating the approaching date for their "*guy*" trip together. He would be shutting down operations for ten days while he was gone but I would continue to take bookings.

This trip obviously meant a lot to him, but at this point in our relationship, I sadly felt he couldn't be trusted. I wanted to tell myself that I was just worrying about nothing, but I knew from what he had done in the past, that he most likely felt he could get away with doing it again. He always had a reason or some crazy story for the photos I had found or texts I had seen and maybe I was just as bad as I continued to allow myself to accept his pathetic excuses. It was wrong, and I continued my downward spiral of drinking whatever I could find at night just to allow myself not to feel anything but emotionally numb.

I started to have thoughts of just going to sleep and not wanting to wake up again to deal with the overwhelming sense of pain and anxiety I felt. My heart raced constantly, and I struggled with fear, sadness, depression, and sleeplessness. These were telltale signs of posttraumatic stress disorder or PTSD. I didn't know what was happening to me, but I did know I was going down a dangerous path. On one occasion, I had severe stomach pains and numbness in my arm. I thought I might be having a heart attack, and Joe had rushed me to the hospital.

After having an MRI done, the doctor told me he really wasn't sure what it could have been except maybe chronic indigestion. I was a healthy person and never had any digestive issues. Everything seemed normal on paper, except that my blood pressure was still slightly high, but I was told it may have been caused by my indigestion. Of course, I didn't talk to the doctor about anything else I had been going through. How could I? I'd been lied to, disrespected, and blamed so many times that I came to always expect the worst. I just forced myself to smile and pretend that everything was okay.

Once Joe left for New Zealand with Shane, I kept myself busy with packing and cleaning, anticipating our move to our new home, located in the same quaint neighborhood as our rental. We had quickly sold our home back in Phoenix and were now a week away from closing escrow on a one-acre property; however, the home needed many repairs to bring it up to date. It would be a challenge, but it would be ours, and we saw the potential of what it could be with a little blood, sweat, and tears.

There were days that Joe must have gotten some sick pleasure of humiliating me in front of my broker, who on many occasions while on a conference call with her, had to listen to him belittle me if things weren't going fast enough or going his way. On one particular call, she heard him yelling at me at the top of his lungs, berating me so badly, that she had to get on the phone with him directly to explain the home buying process as he dismissed everything I had told him. He had left me in tears from that experience.

He got even more upset when I had tried standing up for myself, explaining to him that I didn't tell him how to do his tour rides, so he shouldn't tell me how to do my job as a real estate agent. I had been representing buyers and sellers for thirteen years, and he only left me feeling like he didn't appreciate any of the hard work I had done. My broker was even in disbelief on the way he reacted to a normal real estate transaction. After that whole experience, I vowed to myself that I would never represent him in any transaction, regardless of how much in commissions we would save. It wasn't worth it.

For the moment, I was happy Joe had left with Shane as I desperately needed the space to just breathe and recover from his relentless need to manipulate and control me. He had called me the first night he arrived in New Zealand, telling me how he and Shane were sharing a cabin together and would be going on a training flight first thing in the morning. I sensed his excitement, and for a moment, I felt there was more to the details of his trip there than he was letting on.

He seemed the happiest when Shane was around, laughing and joking and sharing stories about who knows what as I had caught them more than once whispering to one another, wondering why they were being so secretive. It reminded me of how teenage boys would act instead of two grown men. I tried reminding him about the close of escrow on our home but was only met with an apathetic attitude. "I don't have time for this. I have to go, Renee." What was so damn important that he had to get off the phone while I was trying to make sure that the close of escrow went smoothly? "Do you even care about this Joe? Why are you acting like you don't?"

I could tell he had not prepared to speak with me about our home purchase as he quickly lashed out, "I don't care if we close or not. I'm sure things will be fine with closing, and you need to handle it. You're the agent!" *Wait, had he just told me that I could handle it? After the hell he put me through over this purchase and with my broker?* I couldn't believe my ears, but then again, he liked playing these types of mind games with me. All I could think of was he must have wanted to get me off the phone badly enough so he could spend his downtime with Shane. No surprise there.

At the end of the week, we thankfully had closed escrow with no hiccups, and I received a few texts from him when he was getting ready to fly home. I was still packing boxes and moving items to our new place when Joe arrived. As he walked in the door and our eyes met, a sickening feeling washed over me as his eyes told me all that I needed to know. I knew at that exact moment that he had been unfaithful on his trip. His eyes, unlike his mouth, could not lie. He looked away and didn't even approach me with a hug but instead walked into our bedroom with his suitcase. I stood in silence in the middle of our living room and knew that our marriage was in turmoil.

I felt nauseated as I had many times in these situations. I heard him turn on the shower as I walked into the room and saw his phone lying on the bed. I couldn't help but look to see if my gut feeling had been right. As I went through his photos, I saw pictures of the plane that he had flown in, and as if I had already known I would find something, there it was. Pictures of two pretty girls that were part of his flight training. They were wearing cut off shorts and low-cut blouses, which exposed their bare cleavage.

They looked to be in their mid-twenties. As I looked at the texts between him and Shane, I noticed that Shane had made reference to buying a home there so they could come out once a year and have their fun, and I knew then that he wasn't talking about flying. Hearing the shower shut off, I threw his phone back on the bed and stood at the bedside frozen by this man who had deceived me one too many times. It's like the old saying, *"Fool me once, shame on you, but fool me twice, shame on me."*

Of course, I felt he had most likely been unfaithful more than twice. As he opened the bathroom door and saw me standing there, I could tell by the puzzled look he gave me that he knew that I had found out his dirty little secret. I turned to walk out the door and continued packing up our belongings as hardly a word had been spoken between us. I wanted to run far away. I needed to breathe again. I started to question why I stayed with this man. I knew he would come up with some ridiculous lie if I even confronted him about what I had found. I was trapped in a labyrinth of his lies and tried to make sense of it all.

I decided to get checked by my doctor to make sure I had not contacted any STDs. Joe could have been with a number of people over the years, and I was just so naïve to it all, except for what I had found on his phone. Thankfully, all of the tests came back negative. By then, I felt like giving up, but there was also a part of me that felt I needed to fight for my own happiness. I didn't want to be the one to break up our family, and I didn't want to go through another divorce, feeling as if I had failed and hadn't tried hard enough to make things work. I just didn't see it then that the man I had married would never change his deceiving ways and that I was tolerating his behavior by staying in the relationship.

Chapter Twenty-Four

Shameless

It dawned on me that Emma and I had never taken a mother and daughter trip together, and I knew that she was tired of hearing Joe's foul mouth and outrageous behavior. She could see my suffering and had pleaded with me on several occasions to leave Joe. I found myself thinking about it, now more than ever after, as I started to realize that anything would be better than being with someone who treated me this way. What always stopped me was Callie. What would happen to her? She already had a mother who was torn from her life, and if I left, I would be responsible for another one abandoning her.

What was worse, was I couldn't shake the sickening feeling that Joe and Shane were more than just friends. It was a terrible thing to think but my gut feeling told me that he may have explored that experience. It would explain a lot of things and why he always wanted to be with Shane at every given moment. All he did was talk about Shane. Even my brother, who is an openly gay man, said that judging by Joe's actions, he sounded like he was gay. His exact words were, "No one chooses a friend over their own wife unless they are gay."

To further confirm my suspicion, I had recently bumped into Tina at the grocery store. She and her husband, Brad, owned the helicopter tour company, and I had felt an instant connection with her, almost as if our lives were somehow parallel. She and I chatted like we had known each other forever, and eventually, she had confided in me about her troubles at home with Brad, which led me to confide in her about mine. I had needed a friend to talk to, and it was the first time in a long time that I felt I could let down my guard.

I had poured out my heart to her along with all my fears and doubts I had about Joe, including his recent behavior and his feelings for Shane. At that moment, she shared with me that Shane had apparently gotten in between her and Brad in the same manner as he had with Joe and me. Why would Shane do that? I wondered if Shane's wife was even aware of his uncanny behavior.

I needed to get away, and I found it to be the perfect time to take Emma to the upcoming Rolex Three-Day Event in Kentucky, which was one of the largest equestrian competitions in the world. We had watched the televised event every year and had always thought it would be fun to attend in person someday. That someday was now. It was perfect timing and just what we needed at the moment. I needed to be far away from Joe to even think straight. I couldn't tell him yet that I wanted out of the marriage. I wasn't sure how to. I no longer felt love for this man as all I could see when I looked at him now was the devil in disguise.

Emma and I found it exciting to plan our trip together to Kentucky. We planned on taking some horse farm tours while we were there, which would give us a close-up look at the world's premier Thoroughbred horse farms. I wasn't going to ask Joe if I could go as I would have done in the past. I was going to tell him I had already booked the airfare and event tickets, and if he was to give me any grief, I had plenty of ammunition to use from his secret escapades, including his recent trip to New Zealand. Since Emma was getting older, I couldn't help but think it would be one of the most highlighted experiences that we would share together before she went off to college. She deserved this. She had helped so much with Callie and even Hannah at times since she was the oldest, and she did her best to ignore Joe's condescending attitude.

He disregarded her most of the time now, not even acknowledging her or asking how her day at school was when she walked in the door. She would just walk to her room and close her door. It hurt my heart to think he could be that way to her. Sometimes, he would ridicule her just to get at me. I had watched him one day outside as he told Emma to take the trash bin to the curb. She knew she had to do it, as she did every week, so she had told him she would get to it later as trash didn't get picked up until the next morning. That simple response set him off on a tangent.

"You need to take the trash out now!"

That's when I stepped in. "Joe, Emma said she will take it out in a bit. She's trying to finish her homework first. It doesn't need to be taken out right this minute." He looked at me as if I had said that to challenge him somehow.

"The trash needs to be empty! Nothing is done around here! I have to do everything myself!" He grabbed the kitchen trash, which I had just emptied, and took it outside.

"Where are you going with that? There's nothing in it, Joe. I just emptied it." He continued to walk away, raising his hand high enough for me to notice that he had given me the finger. I was so repulsed by his behavior that it only validated my reasons for wanting to leave him. He ended up taking the trash to the curb because he wouldn't have someone else telling him it could be done later. He walked back inside, but this time, something in me said to stand up to his bullying and stop being his punching bag.

"Why the hell would you feel the need to flip me off? What did I do to deserve that?" I believe he was surprised that I hadn't just walked away and not said anything more.

"What are you talking about, Renee? I didn't flip you off! You must be seeing things! It just goes to prove you're crazy!"

That was his answer? I wondered if he realized how crazy he sounded. We both knew he was lying, and I couldn't help but say, "Oh, that's original, Joe. I think you better think of some new material because you continue to say the same thing all the time. How about this—You're the crazy one and you need serious help! By the way, Emma and I have booked a trip to the Rolex Three- Day Event in Kentucky so you will have to stay at home and take care of Callie and run your business for five whole days by yourself. You won't be able to go out whenever you want unless of course, you find another babysitter."

I walked away with an overwhelming sense of empowerment, turning around in time to witness the look of shock suddenly appear across his face, as I slammed the door to our bedroom. I was anticipating the evil rage that was about to be thrown in my direction; however, I heard the television go on in the living room. The pounding in my heart started to fade as I realized that he wasn't coming after me with his violent rage and verbal intimidations. This was different this time. Normally, in a situation like this, he would have unleashed his rage. What had changed? Sadly, I still expected the worst was yet to come, but instead, as he came to bed later that evening, I was shocked by his words.

"I think it's great if you and Emma go to the Rolex event. You both should spend some time together. I'll give you some money for the trip since I know the hotel and car rental will add up." What Joe didn't know is that the trip had already been paid for as my father had offered to pay for it since he knew that I wasn't getting a salary or any kind of income for running Joe's business. I couldn't think of anything to say except, "Thank you, Joe. Emma and I really need this time together. She's getting older and will be off to college soon anyway."

I suddenly thought that maybe he was trying to get rid of me so he could do something with Shane without any fear of me finding out. Callie would have certainly told me if she were to see him with anyone, but at this point, I wouldn't have put it past him. What I really wanted to say was that I wanted time away from him so I could come to terms with what I needed to do, but of course, I couldn't say that directly to him. I was too scared of the consequences, not just from him, but from how I would find a way to leave him. Where would I go? What would I do for work? How could I survive?

I needed to have some kind of income to live on my own, and I wanted Emma to be in a safe environment. I knew the first step would be to somehow convince him that I needed something for myself. Something I could do part-time that wouldn't interfere with running his business. I started to keep my eyes open online for part-time jobs; however, in a small town, there wasn't much of a selection. I had to keep my faith in believing that something would eventually come my way.

At the end of the month, Emma and I left for our trip. As we departed the plane to get to our connecting flight, I saw that I had ten missed calls from Joe. I thought something had happened, so I called him immediately. There was no greeting from him. Just, "Why isn't this reservation system working right? I'm getting calls from people saying they tried to book on our website, and it won't allow them to continue the booking process." Now, I know that he could have easily called the reservation company that we used on the site and spoken to them, but instead, he had called me over and over.

I already knew what he was doing. He was trying to make me feel bad for leaving even after he told us to have a great time. How dare he? After all the times he had gone somewhere and done who knows what with someone else, he had the audacity to play this childish game with me? "Joe, I haven't had a problem with the reservation system, so if you are now, you need to call technical support with the company directly and figure out the problem with them. That's what they're there for. Don't put this on me, especially when you know I'm not there. I have to go. My connecting flight is now boarding." I guess he had not expected me to tell him what he needed to do as he just hung up the phone.

Emma had heard the whole conversation, and said, "Good, I'm glad he hung up. He seriously doesn't know how to do anything without you there. Don't answer if he calls back, mom. He's just going to make you feel bad for going on this trip." For as young as my daughter was, she was smart and could see through his façade of acting so supportive of our mother-daughter trip. She was right, but Joe could still make me feel guilty for the smallest things.

I put it all aside and focused on the itinerary for the next few days. The first day was filled with dressage events, followed by some wonderful horse farm tours, which was the highlight of our trip. The second day was the cross-country event, which was amazing to see up close and personal. You could feel the rush of excitement coming from the oohs and awes of the crowd. The final day was the jumping competition in a grand arena. The beauty and grace of these spectacular horses and their riders were unparalleled to watching it on television.

Being there in the thick of it all was a dream come true. Emma and I knew we would never forget those three glorious days. Joe had not even tried contacting me once. I had tried calling him when we had first arrived and checked in at the hotel, but he had brushed me off, saying that he was too busy to talk to me. I knew he was mad but to make me feel bad for going on a trip with my daughter was even beneath him, or so I thought at the time. What I didn't really understand then was that he had always used this type of tactic to manipulate and control me.

A part of me didn't want to return home. Over the last few days, I thought about contacting a divorce attorney, but then thought we should try marriage counseling. I really didn't want to leave the marriage knowing that I hadn't tried everything that I could to save it. I had to try, even as sick as it made me to think of the things Joe had done. I knew I needed time to look for a job that could provide me with enough income so that I could make it on my own if I had to leave.

Once we returned home, Joe started to take over more of the phone calls and bookings, which offered me some relief. As if he sensed my lighthearted mood, he suggested we go out for a date night. At this point, I was used to Shane always showing up, and I was tired of it. So, I politely asked, "Is Shane going to be there?"

I really expected him to say yes and knew I was in for a lonely evening since the two of them would be chatting all night long, but instead, he replied, "No, Shane isn't coming. It's a date night, and it's just going to be you and me. There's a wine bar in town that has a cover band playing popular eighties songs. I thought you would like it. I need to know if you want to go because I have to buy the tickets now to reserve a table." This was new to me. Was he trying to make an effort to be with just me or did he sense that I wanted to leave him? I wasn't sure.

I wondered if he had felt that he was losing some sort of power over me, but it really just came down to him wanting to have sex, which we hadn't in quite a while. In her book, "Understanding the Sociopath: Why antisocials, narcissists and psychopaths break the rules of life[4]," author Donna Andersen mentions that sociopaths are motivated by three things: *power, control, and sex.* I now know that Joe was capable of doing anything to get it. I asked him again, "So, are you sure Shane's not going because I heard you talking to him on the phone about our date, and I would like it to be just you and me. It hasn't been just you and me on a date together in a long time."

"Of course, Renee. It will be just the both of us, okay?" After everything this man had put me through, I still believed he was telling me the truth, at least that it would just be the two of us for our date night. If he wanted Shane to go, why wouldn't he just tell me? He had no problem telling me when he was going to Shane's house or on trips with him. Why not now? So, I believed what he said.

We left that night and for the first time in a long time, it felt good to just be together. He held my hand on the car ride to the wine bar. We talked about something funny Callie had said and kept our conversation on the kids. I had wanted to talk to him about Hannah but refrained from it as it had concerned me when she had come out for her last visit. Joe was still trying to get Hannah to move in with us full time, and I believe he had Christy thinking about it since Hannah seemed to be mingling with the wrong crowd at school.

Joe continued to press Christy about it, but one day, sitting by the community pool, Hannah had told me that she didn't want to move in with us. "Hannah, your dad wants the best for you and is concerned about your grades and the people you hang around. Maybe you can just try to move up here and see how it goes for the remaining school year. You may end up really liking it here, and I know you love being around Emma and Callie. I think the change would be great."

Her ambiguous reply caught me off guard. "I will never move up here or move in with you guys because I know how my dad is." I had never known that she felt this way, and she had confided in both Emma and me quite often about her feelings, but I knew what she meant. "Emma, your dad loves you. You know that. He would never do anything to hurt you." Deep down in my heart, a part of me questioned whether that was true after some of the terrible things he said about her in the past, but Hannah was only speaking her mind. It was sad to think that Joe had made his own daughter feel this way.

I thought better of it to mention anything to Joe. He would find out in his own way that Hannah wanted to stay with her mother. We arrived at the wine bar, and as he looked for a parking space, I noticed a truck parked upfront that resembled Shane's. My heart started to race as I looked at Joe and asked, "Is that Shane's truck? Is he here?" His eyes started to glaze over as he shrugged. "I don't know. Don't look at me like that. I didn't know he was going to be here. It's just a coincidence. I never asked him if he was coming to this."

I could feel that the night had already been ruined by his words. I knew Shane was there, all the while Joe trying to convince me that he didn't know he was going to be there. As we walked inside to check-in, we were assigned a table. I wasn't surprised when we approached the table to see Shane and his son sitting there. I became angry with another one of his many lies. He had done this on purpose, but why? To humiliate me or to show Shane that he liked playing these mind games?

I couldn't believe he purchased the tickets knowing that Shane must have purchased his at the same time. He had planned this; otherwise, we would have all been assigned to a different table at the time the tickets were purchased. I felt sick as he continued to try and tell me that it was just a coincidence. "No, Joe, it's not. Maybe with showing up for this concert but it's not a coincidence when we are assigned at the same table together. How stupid do you think I am?" People had turned to look at us as I rushed to the bathroom to contain my tears. I just wanted to go home. I felt defeated once more.

As I came back to the table, Joe was gone. I looked at Shane and all I could see was a snake in the grass. "Where did Joe go?" He leaned back in his chair and whispered, "He left. He took an Uber back home." I ran to the parking lot, and my car was still there but clearly, Joe had left. Why did he leave? To continue his sick game? I quickly drove home, trembling with fear, trying to make sense of what had just happened, knowing there would be a vicious confrontation that surely awaited me.

Chapter Twenty-Five

Love and Hate

I couldn't control the overwhelming feeling of needing to vomit as I walked in the door. I could see Joe coming towards me with a fixated look of fury. As my eyes locked with his, I saw something dark and sinister that deeply frightened me. He was hell-bent to make his voice heard, shouting obscenities at the top of his lungs, as he brought his face inches from mine. He pulled me into the bedroom, his fists angrily hitting the door, as he proceeded to act out with a fueled rage.

How dare you embarrass me in front of Shane and his son! We are done! Get the fu** out of my house! I want a divorce!" I could hear Emma's footsteps coming down the hall as she glanced at Joe in disgust. He turned towards her with intense hatred as he said, "Your mother always thinks I'm cheating on her and she's fu***** crazy, always making things up to make me look like I'm a bad husband, but she doesn't realize how good she has it!" Why was he saying anything to Emma about this? Maybe it was the way she looked at him or maybe it was his guilty conscience reacting to something he thought she was aware of.

While Emma and I were in Kentucky, I had finally told her about the photos of other women I had found on Joe's phone and that I was thinking of leaving. She needed to know, and she was old enough now to understand. However, she knew I was hesitant to act on anything because of Callie and what she might endure if we left. He must have suspected that Emma knew, but of course, he was just looking for something to be mad at me about so he would have a reason to file for divorce.

Emma walked to her room as she shouted, "Maybe you shouldn't have other photos of women on your phone then!" Joe spun around as he lashed out angrily. "What did you say to me?" I could tell he was ready to lunge in her direction as he followed her to her room and tried kicking her door open. It's none of your business what's on my phone! You act like a spoiled little princess, and you make me sick!"

As he started to enter her room, my motherly instinct kicked in as I grabbed his arm to pull him away from her door enough so she could lock it. I had never been this scared of him as Emma shouted, "Get out of my room!" I continued to pull him back towards me with what strength I had as I heard her door slam and lock. I was relieved for the moment, but I could hear Callie crying in her room. I wanted to console her, but Joe had spun around, grabbing me so hard, that I cried out in pain. He countered back with an ear-piercing scream, finding a sick sense of joy in my suffering, as he mocked my pain.

At that moment, I wasn't sure what he was capable of as I suddenly thought about his gun in his safe and became frightened. I had my phone in my pocket and quickly tapped my emergency contact, which was my father. While Joe was still on his violent rampage and hurling every type of obscenity my way, my father listened to all of the vulgar things that were being said. Joe continued to talk about divorce and telling me to get out of *his* house or he was going to change the locks and how I would never be able to return to get any of my things.

Thankfully, I knew my rights. "I'm not going anywhere, Joe. You can't just throw me out of the house. We are married, and if you change the locks, I will call the police and they will tell you the same thing. Better yet, go ahead and call the police. I recorded your violent rage for the past forty-five minutes, and I have bruises starting to form on my arms from your hands forcefully grabbing me. I can press charges so you better think real carefully. Oh, and in case you want to try and make everyone believe that I'm crazy, my father heard you on the phone and now knows who you really are."

I don't know what had come over me, but I somehow felt the Renee that had been buried for far too long had suddenly come back from the grave. Not completely, but I had finally stood up to this man who was supposed to be the one to love and protect me. The only person he had ever loved and protected was himself. As if I had knocked some kind of sense into him, he walked away and stayed on the couch. I locked the bedroom door, and after what seemed like forever, I crept over to Callie's room and peeked inside. She had fallen asleep, but I could see the stains on her cheeks her tears had left behind.

I knew she had heard everything. It was hard not to with the sound of his screams that permeated the entire house. I felt terrible for her. I called my father back. He had been beside himself, worrying if Emma, Callie and I were okay. "Renee, you need to get out of that house. I can't believe some of the things he called you. That man is a piece of trash! He doesn't deserve you. Do you want me to fly out there? I will give that sad excuse for a man a piece of my mind!"

My poor father. I didn't want him to worry or be involved but I knew he would be a witness to what had been said if Joe ever tried to turn things around on me in a court of law. He had a way of making people feel sorry for him, even me when I first met him, and I bought his sob stories hook, line, and sinker. "No dad, I'll be okay. I just needed you to hear who he really is so you believe me and know that he's not the great guy you think he is. He's a manipulative person that only wants to control me, and what he did tonight at the wine bar was only a sick mind game, where I believe he just wanted to get me upset, so he had an excuse to behave like a tyrant."

It took some convincing for my father to not board a flight right then and there, feeling the need to pound some sense into Joe. The confrontation wouldn't have worked anyways knowing Joe would never change, but I needed to take care of this myself. Lying in bed that night, unsure of what the next morning would bring, I was suddenly aware of the tears cascading down my face as I wondered how I could ever have loved someone that could be so calculating and evil. Sleep finally took over, but I was awakened an hour later by a rattling sound next to my bed.

As I turned over, I saw Joe standing over me. He had my cell phone in his hand and quickly unplugged it from its charger on my nightstand. He rushed out of the bedroom as my adrenaline kicked in. I jumped up and chased after him through the house. I was not going to go down without a fight. "Give me back my phone!" I grasped it, trying to pry his fingers off until I was on the floor. He had done this before, and he knew I had recorded his vicious outbursts earlier. Even if he had taken my phone, I had changed my password on it so he wouldn't have been able to erase the recording. However, I believe his goal was to destroy my phone so I couldn't retrieve it at all.

"If you don't give me my phone, I will have Emma call the police right now, and all they have to do is look at me and know that I've been assaulted by you." The bruises on my arms had become much more apparent. You could distinctly tell that they were caused by his fingers firmly grasping my arms. He was strangely quiet, attempting to look the other way as if ignoring the inevitable. An odd feeling washed over me, knowing that he didn't want to look directly at me.

As if flipping a light switch, he suddenly went calm and handed me my phone. "We should go to marriage counseling, and if we don't, I will file for divorce. This just isn't going to work." I couldn't even wrap my mind around the fact he would want to go to marriage counseling after all that he just said to me. Why would he want to save our marriage? He had lied so many times that I wasn't even sure if he was flat out lying to me again. Why did he need me here? Wouldn't it have been easier for him if we just divorced?

But ultimately, he just wanted power and control, and of course, sex. I wasn't giving that to him, and we hadn't been intimate in some time. So, I could only imagine that he was having sex with someone else, suspecting what I did about him. I had felt something was going on when he would come home late and take a two-minute shower. My gut instinct told me enough and I don't think I could have beared to know who he may have been with. The chance to go to counseling together was enlightening, but I was curious to know what a therapist would have to say.

Would he see through Joe's charm and charisma? I wondered. I wanted answers but I still needed to find a job, so the next morning, I had a heart to heart with Emma. "It's just a matter of time before things get even worse. I don't believe counseling will change how Joe is. There is something wrong with him. He has a rage inside of him that could potentially escalate even more if provoked and I no longer trust him or what may happen. I need to get a job and start looking for apartments so you can continue to go to school and be free of this toxic environment. I am trying to do what I can, but I also know that Callie is going to be affected by this, which makes it extremely difficult. I'm not even sure if Joe would allow me to be in her life if I left."

Looking dazed and confused by what had happened the night before, Emma whispered, "I called Ryan last night and he almost came up here to protect us from Joe, but I told him to stand by." I felt awful for exposing my own children to this vicious shell of a man and now knowing that my son was scared that something might happen to us.

All because Joe had cleverly masked himself as my soulmate, and sadly, all I could now see was pent-up anger and intense hatred in this man. I was terrified as I prayed to God for help and asked, "Why would you let a man like this come into my life? I don't deserve this. All I have ever wanted was to be loved and happy. What lesson am I supposed to be taking away from this? I don't feel safe any longer, especially with Emma in this environment, and I fear Callie being left alone here with him. God, what do I do?"

I'm not sure why but I immediately felt a sense of calm after that, and even though I had searched that day's job listings, something told me to look at it again. I had been looking every day, but just then, I noticed that a local upscale resort in the area was looking for an assistant manager in their restaurant. I had some management experience twenty years prior and thought, well, they probably won't hire me based on my resume since it's been so long, but I applied anyway and was immediately called in for an interview. The grounds of the resort were breathtaking, and for some reason, I felt comfortable there, almost a calling so to speak, as if I needed this bit of independence.

I had never even known the resort was there as it was tucked back into the mountainside but was still close proximity to town. I looked forward to working, just so I could get away from the overwhelming toxicity at home. Due to the amount of time that had elapsed from my restaurant days, I thought the resort would eventually hire someone else, but to my surprise, I was hired part-time with a schedule that offered flexible hours in the evenings.

This was a well-respected establishment, and I was warmly welcomed by the food and beverage staff. A new job meant shopping for black slacks as part of the required uniform. Joe was aware I had gone on the interview and seemed fine with me working while still handling the majority of his bookings. I had also found a marriage therapist who was male so that Joe would attempt to be forthcoming in our counseling sessions as I knew that he wouldn't listen to anything a female therapist would have to say.

The marriage therapist wanted to meet with us separately first so he could evaluate what each of us wanted out of the marriage. He had no idea what Joe was even capable of, and I wondered if he would see through all of his lies that I'm sure he would likely dream up. I went shopping with Emma the next day to find clothing for my new job. It felt so good to know that I would be getting a paycheck and not solely relying on Joe for every little thing.

I had worked so long for him that I forgot what it felt like to make my own money. On the drive home, Emma and I stopped for lunch. My phone started to ring, but I didn't see the caller ID until we were leaving. I had six missed calls from Joe. Annoyed at wondering what was so important, I called him. "I can't handle this, Renee. The phones are ringing off the hook. How long are you going to be gone? I've got so much going on." What exactly did he have going on? He always made it sound like he was busier than everyone else in the world.

"I'll be home in twenty minutes, Joe, then I'll take the phones." I could tell he was frustrated as he tried to make me feel bad because I wasn't there to help him. I hung up, more annoyed than anything. He continued to call me over and over the rest of the ride home but I didn't answer. There was nothing I could do until I arrived home. I walked in the door, and to my surprise, he wasn't there. I called him. No answer, so I text him. *"I'm home now. I thought you were here. I'll take the phones now."* He responded,

"That's okay. I don't need you to answer the phones anymore."

It quickly dawned on me that he was back to playing his sick little mind games. It was just another day in the life of Joe. What was wrong with him? He wanted to get a reaction out of me, and he liked causing friction between us. I can only imagine that he was with Shane that day. I was at my breaking point; hence, it's sad to say that this man drove me there, all the while enjoying the havoc he wreaked on the people that were closest to him. Shane was the exception.

Once home, I heard Joe rummaging around in the kitchen followed by the pop of a cork being removed from its bottle. No hello or any kind of answer on where he had gone that day. He proceeded to hand me a glass of wine and turned on the television. I stayed silent as he gave me a once-over and said, "Let's watch a movie." I could only think he was trying to avoid me asking where he was that day and what his reasoning had been for making me rush home for nothing. Turning the tables on me, he started fishing for more details about my new job.

"So, I guess Callie and I will have to eat boxed macaroni and cheese since you'll be working mostly nights now." Shaking my head, I replied, "I guess so. Maybe you can go to Shane's house and have dinner. You do that a lot now anyway, and you were supportive of me getting a job so stop with the guilt trip." I wasn't going to let him make me feel bad for something I finally felt good about doing for myself. "I don't go to Shane's every night, Renee. I want to know what kind of uniform you're going to wear at this place."

If I didn't know better, I would have sworn he was jealous. "Why does it matter to you? Don't you trust me?" I couldn't help but ask him that as he had said that to me so many times when I accused him of cheating, such as the times I had found text messages or photos on his phone. The direction of our conversation had turned, and he didn't like it. The resort had a fine dining restaurant and lounge area that catered to high-end clientele, so our uniforms were a tailored long-sleeve, button-down shirt, with black slacks and closed-toed shoes. What did he think that I would be doing?

"What are you going to be wearing, Renee? Let me guess. You're going to try and get good tips so you're probably planning on wearing a low-cut tank top and removing your wedding ring, right?" Of all the things he could have said, but what was I expecting at this point? Truthfully, not much. He could still shock me with his words, but this time I had a response that left him with a taste of his own medicine. "No Joe, I'm not you!"

He jumped up. "What do you mean? I don't do that!" I'm not sure what had transpired over the last few days, but I suddenly wasn't as scared to stand up for myself, and it felt good to fight for the woman who had been lost for so long.

"You haven't worn your wedding ring for the last two months, Joe. Do you think I haven't noticed?" As I headed towards the bedroom, he blatantly replied, "I've been doing work on the house! I can't wear my ring when I'm painting!" "Well, you're not painting now." I had challenged him and judging by the look of defeat on his face, I sensed there would be shocking repercussions in the days to come.

Chapter Twenty-Six

He's Living a Secret Life

The following week leading up to our first counseling session felt almost pointless. Joe had been sleeping on the couch, and I had settled in the bedroom. Emma spent much of her time at her friend's house, and Callie started acting out in front of me. I had been in training at the resort that week so I could only imagine what crazy things Joe was filling her head with. On one occasion, Callie had asked me what time I was leaving for work, and I suspected that Joe was waiting for me to leave so he could continue with his shenanigans.

Waking up the next morning, the day had finally arrived. It was Joe's first meeting with the therapist. Two hours later, he returned with a packet of information that he was told to read over. "Thanks to you, we will have homework to do before our counseling session together." Was he really blaming me? He is the one that had suggested going to marriage counseling. This was just another one of his manipulative tactics, and I suspected he was only doing this to make himself appear as the victim since the telltale signs of divorce was inevitable.

He wanted to come out of this as the all-around good guy while painting me as the crazy wife who had accused him of cheating on multiple occasions. I knew he had an ulterior motive. I had been with him long enough to know how he tried to make me look. The thought crossed my mind that maybe I had just been a smokescreen so he could get away with his promiscuous acts and deep-seated rage. No one ever questioned him because no one ever saw or experienced what I did. No one really knew who he was. I had lived in a world of denial, and for years I had been made to feel that everything was my fault.

"I guess you better do the homework then, that is of course unless you don't want to go to the counseling sessions." I expected him to start an argument, but instead, he threw the handful of papers on the table and walked away. I could never predict how he would react from one day to the next. Our therapist was very welcoming and had made me feel comfortable right away. I had needed someone to talk to for so long, but I was scared that he wouldn't understand the emotional havoc Joe had caused in our relationship. I hardly trusted anyone anymore, and I felt he may not understand all of the emotional trauma I had been through.

How did I tell someone that I had never met about Joe's pathological lying, his wild outbursts, my suspicions of infidelity, his relationship with Shane, and the endless emotional abuse I had endured? It was hard to explain it all, as I had held it in for so long and felt that no one would understand the emotional abuse I had suffered at the hands of this man. All I could think to say was, "I have been through a lot with Joe and I know you will be a neutral party in our sessions, but before you meet with the both of us together, you need to know that Joe is a charmer. He will charm the pants off you. Everyone thinks he's this great guy, but there is another side to him that no one sees. Please be aware of that."

He responded with a kind smile. "Renee, just so you know, no one charms me, but I want to know what you want from this marriage? It's going to be difficult but when I'm talking to Joe in our sessions, you can't become angry or interrupt what's being said until I address you, and I have told him the same thing. There will be certain things that I will ask you that may seem foreign on how you both react to your feelings, but this will be a process, and it requires both of you to work at it. Are you willing to do the work?"

I pondered his question, unsure if I even wanted to because I had felt that Joe would never change and was mentally unstable. I still didn't know anything about sociopaths, but I would soon learn who he really was. On our first counseling session together, Joe never even looked me in the eye. I had a sense that he wanted to run out of the room as if he was being cornered with all the uncomfortable questions being asked. It wasn't easy sitting there, listening to his pitiful excuses and the shameless way he lied. The therapist never flinched as I felt Joe reeling him in once he started crying and talking about how his mother had never been a part of his life. He could drum up tears so easily.

Couldn't the therapist see through this? Nothing being said was even truthful, except his story about his mother. When I had my chance to talk, I was interrupted by Joe more than once. I was scared to say too much in fear of what surely awaited me at home if I did. This just wasn't going to go anywhere. How could it with a partner that sat in therapy and lied the entire time? As we stood up to leave, Joe wrote a check for the therapist and waved it in front of my face. "Here's the damn check, Renee! I hope you're happy!"

I really had not expected such a hostile reaction from him regarding payment as we had agreed that we would both pay for marriage counseling. Joe was scheduled to pay him for the week, and me, the next. Now that I was working, he had expected that from me, so I agreed, mainly to buy myself some time to find a place and keep things calm at the house. The therapist had no reaction and only replied, "Thank you." Didn't he see Joe for who he was? I ignored his childish reaction as I walked out of the office building. I was thankful we had driven separate cars, and I knew the rest of the day at home would be filled with silence.

I arrived home to witness Callie crying in her room. "What's the matter, Callie?" I know she sensed that her father and I were not getting along, but she had heard so much, thanks to Joe always shouting at the top of his lungs. "I don't want you to leave, mama, and I don't want sissy to go either. Daddy told me you're not my mom anymore, and he told me to stop calling you mom." It angered me that Joe could even say such a thing to his daughter, but it broke my heart to know she had been told that I wasn't her mother. I really had no custodial rights to her since she was my daughter only through marrying Joe, but she had become my daughter long before that. I loved her, and I knew Joe would never let me see her if I left. It was just a way for him to try and hurt me, but I feared the one that would suffer the most would be Callie. He must have sensed I was going to leave to tell her such an awful thing.

"Let me tell you something, Callie. No matter what anyone ever says to you, including daddy, you know in your heart how much I love you, and I will always be your mom." I felt an overwhelming need to protect her from his malicious ways. "If you leave, can I go with you? I don't want to stay here. I want to live with you and Emma." The emotional impact of that moment brought tears to my eyes. What could I say to her to make everything okay? Let's just see how things work out but I will talk to daddy if I have to leave. I don't want you to worry about anything. You also know my phone number by heart, right?

"Yes, mama."

"Good, so you know you can call me anytime you want to, okay?"

"Okay, mama."

Callie was the only reason for me to even consider staying, but I also knew I would never have a loving relationship with a man who never really knew what love was. A man who was a con artist, a man who was dangerous, and a man who was a master of deception. It was not a way to live and now I feared what he might do. I no longer felt safe, and I had to get away from his toxic behavior. It was emotionally draining, and I was constantly getting sick. I continued drinking in the evenings to take the pain away, wondering who he was with and what he was really doing behind my back.

Joe had previously changed the meeting time for our next counseling appointment due to work, so we were now supposed to meet at ten o'clock that morning. Since we were driving separately, I reminded him of the appointment as I headed out the door. "What the fu**, Renee! I'm in the middle of updating the website for new tours. I can't just leave right this minute!" I was shocked and angry as he was the one who had changed the time with the therapist. "You are the one that rescheduled the time! You know what, Joe? Never mind! Don't go, then. Obviously, I know what's more important to you!"

I slammed the door purposely on the way out, figuring he would probably get in his car and show up right behind me. I was fed up with his abusive behavior. I sat in the therapist's office, venting my frustrations on what had happened while waiting for Joe to come through the door with a vengeance, but he never did. "Well, Renee, it is obvious to me that Joe is not interested in saving this marriage, and knowing what I do from meeting the both of you separately, and then together, I am going to be completely honest with you."

I sat motionless thinking of how many people had probably poured their hearts out and cried in that same spot where I was sitting. Would I be surprised or shocked by his answer? I shook my head, encouraging him to continue.

"I believe Joe is leading a secret life, but I cannot divulge how I know or what was said between him and I. I can only tell you that who you see is who he is. He will never change. Your choice is either to live with that or get out of the relationship. I know the name of a good divorce attorney if you need one."

At that moment, I felt like someone had just smacked me across the face. It was the validation I had been looking for. I needed to leave my husband, knowing things would only get worse if I didn't, but then I thought about Callie.

"What about Callie? I can't just leave her."

"Renee, you need to do what's right for you and stop thinking of everyone else. This is your life, and you only get one."

Just then, I wondered what he knew and what Joe must have told him for him to tell me he was living a secret life. I believe Joe had told the therapist that he wanted to bring

Shane to our next counseling session as I remember him bringing it up and dismissed it as one of his little mind games, but maybe he had told the therapist he wanted Shane there. The thought of the two of them together made me extremely nauseous. It was if someone had just woken me from a deep sleep that I had been in for eight long years.

Granted, the therapist had never said he had diagnosed Joe with an antisocial personality disorder (ASPD) or that he was a sociopath, but medically, sociopath and sociopathy are not true clinical terms that are endorsed by the American Psychiatric Association or any other mental health professional. As far as I knew, he had an undiagnosed mental illness that was incurable. Judging from his expression, I could tell he knew more than he was saying, but I would never know the rest of the story. The very next day Joe filed for divorce.

Chapter Twenty-Seven

Finally Free

Joe and Callie were gone the next morning. It was a school day so I knew he had most likely gone to Shane's house, then taken her to school. I had often wondered what Shane's wife had thought of him always being over at their house; however, I didn't know her that well. I could only imagine the crazy things Joe was filling her head with. He probably had her eating out of the palm of his hand, concocting some wild stories about me so she felt sorry for him. She was a smart woman but if she ever caught a glimpse of the man behind the mask, she would come to know the destruction he was capable of leaving in his path.

The home I had once known had become a stale and toxic environment. Everywhere I looked, I saw Joe. He had never let me decorate the house to my liking. The kitchen had been remodeled to his specifications, from the color of the new cabinets to the granite counters, to the hardwood flooring. If he had ever asked what I thought of something he liked, I was expected to agree with him, otherwise, a terrible argument would ensue, and he would end up purchasing the item anyways. There was not one shred of my personal taste entwined in that house. It was all Joe.

Now looking at everything around me made me feel dirty. He had even taken down picture frames of the children that I had placed in the living room, stating that no one wanted to see photos of the kids when they were little. What kind of person did that? My head was still spinning from what the therapist had said. A part of me was shocked by hearing he was living a secret life, but I had always felt that Joe had people in his life that I didn't know about.

As I powered on my phone, I had an unread text message from Shane. I wasn't sure if I had wanted to read it, but I was curious if Joe had somehow gotten him to do his dirty work. *"Any chance I can bend your ear for thirty minutes? I'm not a counselor but do feel I need to convey some thoughts."*

What was this? Was Shane really expecting me to believe him when he was so tight with Joe? I wouldn't have believed anything he had to say, and this was none of his business. I was tired of him always being in the middle of everything. Nothing was ever private between Joe and me. *"No thanks. He is the one who has threatened divorce, so maybe you should be talking to him. He's your friend, and you're the most important person in his life. He has made that perfectly clear."*

A half-hearted snicker escaped me at the response that followed. *"Friends don't replace wives."* What was Joe doing? Was he scared he wouldn't have someone running his business any longer or a babysitter for Callie? Or maybe he was scared of everyone finding out who he really was.

I could only think to reply, *"Tell him that."* He was quick to respond, *"I have."* I knew from listening to Joe's prior threats that he most likely had a divorce attorney lined up that Shane knew. Following my hunch, I text Shane. *"What's the name of Joe's attorney? I will need to know when I speak to my own attorney."* I waited, curious with what answer Shane would text me, but I didn't have to wait long. *"Her name is Amy D. Banfield."*

I knew that Joe wouldn't go there alone. He would take Shane with him because Joe never liked to do anything on his own. He always wanted someone around, whether it be me, his father, or Shane. I quickly retrieved the attorney's name the therapist had given me and made an appointment with her for the next day. I was thankful that I had to work that night because I didn't want to be anywhere near Joe when he came home.

As I continued my search for rentals, a listing for a townhome in the area caught my eye. It looked to be a newer build as most rentals that I could afford were older properties and outdated. My main concern was that I wanted Emma to feel safe since I was working mainly in the evenings. Somehow, I just sensed that this would be our new place. I called the property manager right away and set up a time to view it. I knew it wouldn't be available for long.

That evening, I was in the middle of training a new employee when a woman approached me in the restaurant lounge. "Hi there. Are you Renee Olivier?" I looked at the envelope she was holding, and I instantly knew what was about to happen. "Yes, I am." She smiled, as she handed me the envelope. "You've been served. Have a nice day." I suddenly felt sick and heard a faint whisper next to me.

"Oh my God. Are those divorce papers?"

"Yes, but I'm not really surprised. I just thought I would be served at home if anything."

"Well, it sounds like your soon-to-be ex-husband is a real tool."

Oh, he had no idea! Joe had done this to humiliate me in front of the people I worked with. My heart was pounding in my chest as I text him. He had wasted no time filing for divorce. *"You had to serve me at work? You could have served me at the house or had just given me the papers."* My phone immediately vibrated as I read his response. *"I didn't want to serve you in front of the kids."*

That was an outright lie. He had yelled at me in front of the kids so many times over the years without feeling any remorse and now he was worried about serving me divorce papers in front of them? Was that his best excuse? *"That's a bunch of crap, and you know it! You did it just to humiliate me in front of people I work with."* He never responded.

Waking up the next morning, I realized Joe had never come home. I knew he was at Shane's and poor Callie was caught in the middle of it all. Emma and I focused on moving as soon as possible, and once we saw the townhome, we knew it was perfect for us. It had all the modern upgrades with an open kitchen and beautiful bay windows. I knew I wouldn't find anything else like it, so I immediately put a security deposit down. It would be available in two weeks.

The current tenants even offered to help us move in. It was a blessing to find such an ideal place, and I prayed the next two weeks would fly by. I wanted to get out of our toxic environment so badly. On the nights I came home from work and pulled into the driveway, the chronic stress of the situation was to such a degree, that I felt the urge to vomit. I would retreat to the bedroom and lock the door. Joe was gone most nights now, but I still feared he may do something entirely crazy when I was asleep. I slept with my pepper spray and my phone under my pillow as it was the only measure of protection that I had.

I had spoken to my attorney about the pre-nuptial agreement we had originally signed. She felt I would be awarded more in financial support without the prenup in place as she believed it was full of mistakes and would most likely be thrown out by the presiding judge. I knew fighting Joe would be a costly uphill battle, and I didn't even want to face him knowing what he was capable of. I advised my attorney that I only wanted what was originally agreed to plus my real estate commissions back since they had gone towards renovations and Joe was keeping the house. I was walking away with hardly anything.

Sadly, I knew I had to sell Kensington as Joe had made it clear with his words. "The horses are now your fu*****responsibility, and I won't be putting another dime towards them!" Leaving me with no way to financially care for them, we ended up retiring our two older horses to good homes but Emma had been so attached to Kensington. He was a part of our family and selling him was one of the hardest things we had to do.

Even though Emma understood and was busy preparing for college, we knew there would be an emptiness in our lives. We were grateful to find a beautiful equine facility that wanted to purchase Kensington as a lesson horse for their students and knew he would be well taken care of. Watching the new owners drive away with him was heartbreaking, but we knew it was the right thing to do and he would be loved by the students there.

Joe reluctantly agreed to reimburse me for my commissions, but since he had to pay that and the financial support he consented to in the prenup, he requested a payment reimbursement over a five-year period. I believed it was his way of feeling he still had power and control over me. My attorney chuckled at the thought of any judge approving such a long payment plan, which was quickly dismissed. After negotiating a realistic schedule, we both agreed to payments over a two-year timeframe. It was done.

The petition for dissolution of marriage had been executed and was filed with the court. I thought I would cry or feel an overwhelming loss of some sort, but instead, I felt like a huge weight had been lifted off of my shoulders. I was finally free of this man and I was ready for a fresh start. Moving day finally arrived, and a few people that had befriended me at work, came by to offer their help with some heavy lifting. Even some of Emma's high school friends from the football team offered their help. We were forever grateful as I'm not sure how we would have conquered it all.

Joe kept a low profile outside, while Callie ran over to Emma and me. There was a huge tug on my heart, as Callie started to cry, pleading with us not to go. Everyone standing there was affected by that moment. I knew I needed to find a way to convince Joe to let me see her once we settled in our new place. Joe's friend, Matt, had flown out from New York and was there to help him with Callie for the time being.

Out of concern, I had asked a friend of mine, who was a parent at her school, to check in on her as Joe refused to allow me to see her at school, stating it would only confuse her. He was only doing this now to hurt me and wasn't thinking of what was best for Callie. It was sad to think that she would be left alone to endure his violent outbursts unless Hannah moved in for the following school year. As we drove away, I looked back to see Callie sitting on the front porch, waving goodbye to us. I couldn't control the tears that followed.

Chapter Twenty-Eight
Healing in the Aftermath

The first week in our new home was filled with the unpacking of boxes and purchasing new furniture. It slowly started to feel and look like home. The first few nights there had been the toughest, as it felt odd not having someone to wake up next too. I often found myself wondering why this had happened. Why did I meet this man?—Why did he take advantage of me?—Why did he hate me so much?—Why wasn't I enough? Why, why, why? I cried a lot, in the beginning, trying to come to terms with it all, wondering what I had done to deserve this.

By the following week, I started to realize how peaceful things were. There was no yelling, no one putting me down, no name-calling, and no mind games. I wasn't left wondering who my partner had been with anymore. That dreaded feeling in the pit of my stomach of being constantly nauseous had gone away. I felt I could breathe again; however, I continued to go through all of the *whys* in my head. I had felt as if someone had died. I mourned the death of my marriage to a man I had been with for eight years. Trying to heal from all of the trauma he inflicted was not easy.

I felt alone, numb, confused, and even hopeless at times. I could still hear his voice in my head telling me that I would come back because I wouldn't be able to live without him. I had been a victim of his abuse and overwhelmed by the past, and I came to recognize the struggles I had been through. A friend of mine that I used to work with happened to call me out of the blue one day. I started to tell her about my divorce and touched on some of the things Joe had done. It felt good to vent to someone. She was shocked by my bizarre story, to say the least, but then said something that no one had ever said to me.

"Renee, what you're describing to me sounds like you were dealing with a sociopath."

I was taken aback by her comment. "A sociopath? He's not a serial killer or anything; he just has a mental illness that really hasn't been diagnosed."

"Just look up the definition of a sociopath. Maybe you'll have some clarification from what you went through. You have pretty much described one and not all of them are serial killers."

I couldn't believe what she was saying. Could it be true? How did I not know this? Why hadn't the therapist mentioned it?

I started to research everything I could find on sociopathy and spent the next few days glued to the internet. My learning curve was massive, and I felt like a million light bulbs had suddenly gone on in my brain. I found a wealth of information and descriptions of people who sounded exactly like my ex-husband. The idea that Joe had a personality disorder and one that is often referred to in today's world as sociopathy absolutely floored me, but it all made sense now. I finally had an answer to who and what he was.

When I think back to those difficult times, I think about how naïve I had been to who this man really was. Why did I not know about this sooner? I learned that anytime I had accused him of infidelity, it was common for him to label me as insecure or jealous to avoid suspicion. I lived through a hell of emotional abuse, lying, cheating, and manipulation. I realized Joe had used a form of mental abuse on me called *"gaslighting,"* which is a hallmark trait of a sociopath, and his manipulation tactics caused me to doubt my own perception, memory, and sanity.

Continuing my research, I was shocked to learn that sociopaths have a very weak conscience and have no emotions of love or fear, which is what makes them master manipulators of their victims. The level of validation this had provided for me was uplifting. I wasn't crazy, and I hadn't imagined it all. I wasn't insecure or jealous as Joe had liked telling me time and time again. I started to realize how lucky I was as I continued to read that some victims never leave this parasitic lifestyle.

It was so easy for others that had never lived this nightmare to say, *"Well, why didn't you just leave if he was being that way?"* I can sum it up in one word. *"FEAR!"* Fear will paralyze you, and a sociopath will play on your deepest fears. It's crippling when you combine that with emotional abuse. It robs a person of their self-esteem and the ability to think rationally. By the time I had identified that there was a real problem with Joe, I had already begun to doubt myself and my own sense of reality, which led me to question my every thought.

To me, it had been a form of psychological torture, and I was made to feel that I needed him to survive. Unfortunately, none of this came to light for me until the end of my marriage, and I was able to break free from the overwhelming fear and emotional abuse I had suffered. I started to slowly heal by confiding with my family and a few close friends that had remained in my life. I reached out to other survivors for support, and I gradually started to love myself again.

It was a painful process, but I slowly started to thrive in my new life, and I stopped blaming myself. Therapy had also helped me understand that my empathy and kindness were my strengths, not my weakness, and not everyone was out there to get me. The Renee that had been buried for so long was resurrected. I was back to my happy, go-lucky self, and I knew Emma was much happier too. Over the next few months, Joe's friend, Matt, somehow convinced Joe into letting me see Callie. For a while, the visits went smoothly, but knowing that any little thing could set him off, it only took Callie crying one night, pleading to come and live with me. All I could do was tell her I would see her soon and maybe I could see her more often if it was okay with her dad.

He sent me a text message shortly after that and told me I could no longer see Callie because she always came home upset and would start crying after being with me. He continued his rant saying that I only spoiled her and he wouldn't have his daughter growing up under those circumstances. I reached out to his friend, Matt, but this time, he couldn't get Joe to change his mind. Joe knew how much I loved Callie.

She still called me mama, so I can only imagine that he wanted to hurt me in any way he could. It saddened me to think he could just tear me away from her life after I had been the only mother she had really ever known. He wouldn't even let me talk to her on the phone. There would be no contact. He wanted to erase me and Emma from her life. Not long after, I received another text message from Matt.

"I'm going back to New York. Joe is seeing some twenty-something in heels who's always at the house. All they do is fight after he loses his temper at the drop of a dime, and I'm tired of hearing it. I don't know how you lived with that man for eight years. In my opinion, he lost

the best thing that ever happened to him. Callie seems to be doing fine, and she's now taking dance classes. I can tell she really enjoys it, but she misses you."

I wasn't surprised that Joe was seeing some young girl in her twenties, but I was happy Callie was pre-occupied with an after-school activity, staying as far away from that toxic environment as possible. I thanked Matt for reaching out, and it had felt good to know that he saw Joe for who he was. He had only been living at the house for a short time and he couldn't even deal with Joe anymore. To me, it only supported the fact that Joe would never change, and Matt had seen a glimpse of the man behind the mask. I only hoped that Callie would be okay and be able to confide in another woman in her life that she trusted. She had even tried a few times to email me from her school email address, but sadly, Joe put a stop to that as well.

Chapter Twenty-Nine

What Goes Around Comes Around

Months had passed and I started to become a happier, healthier, and stronger version of myself than I could have ever imagined. I continued to get updates from my friend on Callie and was happy to hear she was doing well in school. I had thought that maybe one day Callie would call me, and I vowed I would never change my phone number, just in case. I felt happy and content in my new life. Working at the resort had given me a new-found independence and I had made new friends there. I had finally agreed one night to go out with Tina, who had become a close friend. We felt connected somehow as we had shared such similar experiences in our lives.

I was happy most days just being at home or going to work. I really didn't get out much, but I thought a night on the town would be good for me. Even Emma had told me she was happy I was going out with a friend for the evening. Tina had heard there was a cover band playing at a popular bar in town and wanted to go, so I decided to spruce myself up at her house. It had been a long time since I dressed up. Glancing in the mirror, I felt I was looking at the real me again. I felt beautiful and happy I was finally getting out on the town.

Once we arrived, we made our way inside to order drinks. The band had started playing, and out of the corner of my eye, I noticed someone was staring at me. As I turned, a man approached me and asked me to dance. I reluctantly agreed, but as he whirled me to the dance floor, I was caught up in the moment, as if time had stood still, feeling alive and allowing myself to have fun with this nice looking stranger. As we danced, Tina came running up to me. "You'll never guess who is here!"

I turned around and came face to face with Joe. He had been standing there, staring at me, watching me dance with this man. This was one thing I didn't like about living in a small town as there was a greater chance to run into someone you knew. It had looked as if he was there by himself, and I was surprised that Shane wasn't with him since they were pretty much inseparable. After all the things he had done and put me through, I could only think of one word. *Karma!* "Oh, great! Why does he have to be here?" Pulling me aside, Tina said, "Joe just approached me and told me that I should tell you to stay away from that guy you're dancing with. He said he's bad news." I laughed, thinking it must have stung just a little to see me with someone else.

"Really? Well, it's none of his business what I do or who I'm around anymore." For some reason, that experience filled me with a sense of empowerment, and I knew then that he would never be able to break me down again. By the time I turned back around, he was gone. It would be the last time that I ever saw him. I knew that living in a small town, he would always try to find a way to promote conflict. He liked fabricating stories, while trying to damage my reputation, no matter how wrong it was. I no longer felt affected by what he did, said, or thought as I could now see clearly for who he was.

Chapter Thirty

A Fresh Start

I thought I would reach out to Joe once more to see if Callie could attend Emma's high school graduation, but he never responded. I already knew the answer anyways, but I thought maybe there was a chance he would let her since it was for Emma's graduation, but it wasn't to be. I was so proud of my daughter. She was a smart girl who I knew would go far in life. She had also gone through such a dark time but had blossomed into the beautiful young lady that was now receiving her diploma. I admired both Emma and Ryan for their strength and courage.

I thanked God every day for them as they were the best thing that had ever happened to me. Life was beautiful again, and I had taken the time to heal my heart and my mind. After Emma graduated, I had felt the urge to want to move to a different town as I had never really felt that I would call this valley home. It had been forever tainted with bad memories of a failed marriage to someone I had once loved.

About that time, I decided to write down all of the things that I wanted in my daily journal. I wanted a big piece of land, a house, dogs, horses, and a wonderful man to share it all with. A man who would just love me for me. A man I could laugh with, talk to, and ultimately be my best friend. I described his features, even, down to the color of his eyes. I closed my journal, feeling grateful for what I had at the moment and went on with life. My friends had tried on many occasions setting me up on a blind date, but I didn't want to meet anyone that lived directly in town.

Since I was a homebody, I decided to join an online dating site once again, mainly to see what was out there. However, I didn't feel a connection with anyone, and I knew this time what I wanted and believed the right person would come along when the time was right. Two days before my subscription to the dating site was due to expire, a photo of a man caught my eye. Even though he lived a five-hour drive away, something had made me reach out to say hello, and I had commented on how cute his dogs were. I thought that would be the end of it, but to my surprise, he responded saying that the photos of the horses I had in my profile were cute.

He asked if I rode, which turned into a long conversation, and I realized how much we had in common. His name was Noah. He had also been married twice, had children that were Emma and Ryan's age, and grew up riding horses as I had. I instantly felt an attraction and a connection to this man. After talking for hours on end, we decided to meet in person, and I had immediately felt like I had known this man my whole life. He made my heart skip a beat. There was a comfort in just being with him, and I knew that deep down, this man would be in my life forever.

We continued to see one another when we could, and one night, as I opened my journal, I flipped to the page I had written on what I wanted in a partner. I was overwhelmed with emotion as I hadn't even realized that Noah encompassed everything I had written down. Since Emma was going to college and moving out, I was on my own for the first time in over twenty years, and that's when I felt I needed a lifestyle change. Surprisingly, Noah had been thinking about moving back to Missouri where he had grown up as a child. His family had a hundred-acre farm in the country, and we discussed moving there together.

It was a big step, but the timing felt right, and once moving day arrived, it was hard saying our goodbyes to our children. There was a part of me that felt I had lived in a bubble far too long and living in the country would be a wonderful lifestyle change. The other part of me felt guilty for leaving my children, but Emma could see that I was happy and said, "I just want you to be happy, mom. You deserve it." Her love and support was the most beautiful gift I could have asked for.

Noah and I started our new life together in Missouri and one day, looking for properties close to his work, we found our dream home, and only a few months later, we were married. It had taken me half of my life to find the love of my life and not a day goes by that Noah doesn't tell me he loves me. As my father once told me, "The man that's meant for you will fight for you, pick you up when you're feeling down, and will give you their smile when it's hard for you to find yours. They will never get power from seeing you hurt or joy from seeing you cry. The man that's meant to love you will always know what he has."

Final Thoughts

It is often the kindest and most trusting individuals who suffer the most at the hands of sociopaths, and the healing process can continue long after the relationship has ended. Those caught in the wrath of a sociopath are often left wondering, *"What happened to me? Why does this person have such a powerful effect on me?"*

Sociopaths are skilled con artists. They may be the most loving, charming, affectionate, and giving person you have ever met. But it's too good to be true. They can be highly effective at getting you to overlook the warning signs you see or sense. They take you into their confidence, with the goal of getting you to doubt yourself and trust them. They will sweep you up in empty promises full of romance and declarations of love, professing that you are their soulmate. A sociopath is not capable of true love, even though it feels that way in the beginning. That is all part of their monumental plan to gain power and control over you.

You are not their equal, for they are incapable of seeing anyone this way. The reason we allowed the sociopath to affect us, control us, and send us so very low is because we were told by them that they loved us, needed us, and would die if they had to live without us. They will "*gaslight*" you, and it will materialize so unexpectantly with such a grand reversal of truth, that everything else may cease to exist for a while.

They will return to "*love bombing*" intermittently to create a trauma bond that can feel like an addiction that is difficult to quit. It is a powerful reminder of how complex and dangerous a sociopath remains today. The good news is you can heal, and you can learn to trust and love again, rather than feel fearful that life is out to get you at every turn. It'll just take time. Only those who have experienced this madness first-hand can possibly understand what others involved with a sociopath have been through. This is how we heal by sharing our stories. Heed those red flags, and listen to your intuition. I only wished I had paid more attention to mine at the time.

If my story resonates with you by identifying some of these characteristics and you suspect you're with a sociopath, the best thing you can do for yourself is to walk away and never interact with them again. They will never change who they are. It can also be healing to tell your friends and family what you've experienced. I had waited far too long to do so as I thought no one would believe me or truly understand, but in my experience, the people close to you will want to offer their support.

The support system you create will go a long way in helping you recover from this trauma. It's also important to seek professional help. Speak to a therapist or psychiatrist you're comfortable with who specializes in domestic abuse and toxic relationships. Writing your feelings down in a journal can also help make sense of the perplexing disarray you may feel in the moment, especially when you first get back out on your own. The defining moment for me was researching online articles on sociopathy and ASPD, which helped me gain a greater understanding of what I had been subjected to for years.

The purpose of writing my story is to help anyone reading it in identifying if they are in a dysfunctional relationship, not to mention, a very dangerous one. I hope by speaking about my experience, I can be an example for others. Please reclaim your life by standing up against anyone who takes away from your happiness. Life is too short to not be happy and you deserve that.

Resources

When I initially started researching sociopaths and the recovery process, I found the following books and websites extremely helpful and informative. They validated what I had gone through for years and offered a world of support in learning how to heal from that experience. I have listed them below by title in alphabetical order.

Healing from Hidden Abuse: A Journey Through the Stages of Recovery from Psychological Abuse by Shannon Thomas, LCSW

In Sheep's Clothing: Understanding and Dealing with Manipulative People by George Simon, Jr., PhD

Out of the Fog: Moving from Confusion to Clarity After Narcissistic Abuse by Dana Morningstar

Red Flags of Love Fraud: 10 Signs You're Dating a Sociopath by Donna Andersen

The Sociopath Next Door by Martha Stout PhD

Understanding the Sociopath: Why antisocials, narcissists and psychopaths break the rules of life by Donna Andersen

Whole Again: Healing Your Heart and Rediscovering Your True Self After Toxic Relationships and Emotional Abuse by Jackson MacKenzie

Without Conscience: The Disturbing World of the Psychopaths Among Us by Robert D. Hare, PhD

https://blogs.psychcentral.com/

https://lovefraud.com/

https://www.talkspace.com/blog/what-is-a-sociopath/

Endnotes

1 Martha Stout, The Sociopath Next Door, New York, NY: Three Rivers Press, 2006.

2 Donna Andersen, Red Flags of Love Fraud: 10 Signs You're Dating a Sociopath, Egg Harbor Township, NJ: Anderly Publishing, 2012.

3 Shahida Arabi, **7** Gaslighting Phrases Malignant Narcissists, Sociopaths and Psychopaths Use to Silence You, Translated: Psych Central: Blog: Recovering From a Narcissist, 2019.

4 Donna Andersen, Understanding the Sociopath: Why Antisocials, Narcissists and Psychopaths Break the Rules of Life, Egg Harbor Township, NJ: Anderly Publishing, 2019.

About the Author

Renee Olivier knows the pain and chaos that accompanies toxic relationships and has found the beauty on the other side of brokenness. As a victim of sociopathic violence, she hopes her story will offer a sense of empowerment in helping other victims of emotional abuse break their silence.

She recently married the love of her life and lives with her husband and their three dogs in the beautiful Missouri countryside. For more information or to contact her directly, please visit www.ReneeOlivier.com.